Just a Breath Away

Tell Me How to Die,
I've Never Done This Before

Just a Breath Away

Tell Me How to Die,
I've Never Done This Before

By Rev. Edward N. Tabbitas

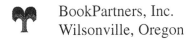

BookPartners, Inc.
Wilsonville, Oregon

Cover design by Richard Ferguson
Text design by Sheryl Mehary

BookPartners, Inc.
P.O. Box 922
Wilsonville, Oregon 97070

I dedicate this book to the Creator God for enhancing my courage to move beyond my fears into the world of spiritual communication.

Acknowledgments

I am deeply grateful to my wife, Prudence, and my children, Philip, Anthony and Michelle, for their unconditional love and encouragement.

My special gratitude to my parents and all the loved ones who have passed over and allowed me to communicate with them.

Next, I would like to thank all my family and friends for their encouragement. I am grateful to Lisa Sulzer for her dedication of time. I am eternally grateful to Rosemarie Nania for her patience, understanding and unconditional inspiration.

From my heart I am indebted to my guide Running Bear.

A very special thank you to Bill and Nina for giving me the time to travel my life's path.

Also my thanks to Gloria and June for their gentle inspiration.

Finally, I would like to thank Les Mound for her introduction to Thorn and Ursula Bacon. I am very grateful to them for their encouragement and for helping me bring this book to full fruition.

And when he shall die
Take him and cut him out in little stars,
And he will make the face of heav'n so fine
That all the world will be in love with Night
And pay no worship to the garish sun.

William Shakespeare
Romeo and Juliet

Do not stand by my grave and weep.
I am not there, I do not sleep.
I am the thousand winds that blow.
I am the diamond glint in the snow.
I am the sunlight in ripened grain.
I am the gentle autumn rain.
When you awake in the morning hush,
I am the swift uplifting rush
Of quiet birds in circle flight.
I am the soft starshine at night.
Do not stand by my grave and cry.
I am not there. I did not die.

Author Unknown

Table of Contents

Introduction

Tell Me How To Die, I've Never Done This Before

Death for most of us is our last voyage because we believe as we lie on our final bed that we have never died before. Few of us remember our past lifetimes. Yet each of us has taken part in this special ritual many times before.

From the moment we are born until the age of three we have memories of an angelic realm. It is our connection to the angelic realm that prompts us as young children to laugh with, and have conversation with, people who aren't there. Children sometimes claim they have spoken to a grandparent who passed over, one they may have never met on earth.

Beginning around age three, we replace the light of love from the angelic realm with the artificial light of earth. We forget what we learned in the angelic realm, and learn to distrust our neighbors, people of different colors and fear the threats to our lives. Greatest is our fear of dying. Because this is so, it is important for each of us to look at other people for their angelic light. We learn to understand that another person's needs just may be a manifestation of his fears.

As we move on in this life, on this wonderful earth we all share, we must always try to keep in mind that what we do today may come back to us tomorrow. Usually, we come to realize in our final days that we have to make peace, not only with ourselves, but with our loved ones. We believe that God is going to judge our sins. Many of us do not understand that we are given free will by God, and that means we are also given the burden of judging ourselves. Who better than you to judge the things you may have done wrong? If someone else were to judge us, in time the details of our transgressions would be forgotten. But, if you and I examine ourselves, the personal nature of our judgment can last a lifetime. And at the close of your life, you, like all of us, are apt to recall all of the things you have done wrong, as well as the wonderful things you did for others.

And there are those of us who can remember fragments or large portions of other existences in years past.

Sometimes we ask Creator God for things that cannot be, or should not be, and, of course, we are not given them. Many of us have asked to have the life of our loved ones extended. But it was the choice of that loved one prior to his birth to leave the earthplane on the day he did. Many times we blame God for taking a loved one, but do we ever take the time to thank God for bringing that loved one into our lives?

When we say our prayers, each prayer is heard individually, identified and answered. Often, the answer does not come at the moment we would like, or with the result we hoped for, but most certainly when we need a prayer answered, it will be. If the answer does not seem satisfactory, then you must examine it from the standpoint that God has provided you with a solution in keeping with your destiny

It was Joseph and Laurie Braga in their Foreword to Elisabeth Kübler-Ross's book, *Death: the Final Stage of Growth,* who wrote: "All that you are and all that you've done and been is culminated in your death. When you're dying, if you're fortunate enough to have some prior warning (other than that we all have all the time if we come to terms with our finiteness), you get your final chance to grow, to become more truly who you really are, to become more fully human. But you don't need to, nor should you, wait until death is at your doorstep before you start to really live. If you can begin to see death as an invisible, but friendly, companion on your life's journey — gently reminding you not to wait till tomorrow to do what you mean to do — then you can learn to *live* your life rather than simply passing through it."

That is the reason for this book, to show you, through my own experience as a person, and as a minister, how to die with purpose, with a sense of accomplishment, and a strong desire to go forward farther than you have been. First, you must come to understand that life is preparation for death. Death is not the end, ever. But because as corporeal individuals on this earthplane, we have never died before in the body we occupy, we are uncertain, fearful, often depressed and unconvinced that we have a future, that our spirits have a home in a generous domain beyond the scope of our vision.

Every experience I have had as a grief counselor and as a minister who has helped to explain death as I see it to hundreds of people who have lost a loved one, has convinced me that we must never fear death, nor think of it as an ending. Rather, it is the departure point for the next stage of human growth. In this book, I hope to show how many people have come to embrace that belief.

Chapter 1

The Stranger at the Airport

At a dinner party at my house in Staten Island one evening a few months ago, one of the dinner guests, a remarkable woman, told a story about her older sister that fascinated everybody at the table. Here is what she told us about Martha:

Shortly after a thorough medical checkup following her complaint of a sore spot high on her shoulder blade, Martha's doctor asked her to come to his office. As soon as she was seated in a chair in front of his desk, Dr. Claude Burger said to his patient, "Martha, I've never been good at breaking bad news, but the fact is I have some disturbing information to give you."

A little shaken, Martha, a slender fifty-one-year-old mother of three grown children, with a husband she loved and a flower shop she was devoted to, sat a little straighter in her chair. She looked directly into her physician's eyes. "All right, Doctor, what's the matter with me?"

Dr. Burger clasped his hands together on his desk and said, "It's the sore spot on your right shoulder. I could show you on the x-rays we took, if you like, but, well, it's cancerous. And it's the fast-growing kind. Already it's metastasized and that means we can't stop it."

He paused, and Martha leaned forward in her chair. "You're sure about this? I mean, there's no question in your mind that it's fatal?"

"No, Martha, there's no question. I've had five radiologists examine the x-rays and they all agree. Of course, you can ... probably should ... get another opinion...."

"I don't think that'll be necessary," Martha replied. "I trust you. You've always been honest and straightforward with us. How long do I have?"

"It's hard to tell, Martha. I'd say three, maybe four months."

"Oh dear, that soon?"

"Yes."

Martha left her physician's office and drove directly home instead of opening her flower shop in southwest Boston. She phoned her assistant, Laura, at her apartment, and explained she had been delayed. Would Laura open the shop and take care of the pending orders? Martha said the delay might be prolonged. She thanked Laura and sat down in the kitchen and sipped cold breakfast coffee.

She was slightly amazed at her calm. Her death had been predicted by a steady, reliable physician whose eyes had mirrored his distress and sympathy. Four months, probably three, and she would be gone. How could that be? A devout Catholic, who rarely missed Mass, who could quote many passages from the Bible when she chose, Martha was surprised at the emptiness in her head. Certainly, she thought, some profound expression of loss should rise from her mind to console her, but all she could think of was that she had forgotten to take out the kitchen garbage from under the sink.

It was much later that day when George, her husband, came home from his work as a lumber broker that she broke the news to him. After her announcement, when George recovered from the initial shock and finality of the doctor's verdict, the two of them sat subdued, blank-faced and empty of words in their living room.

Martha broke the silence between them when she said she had decided not to tell their children about her shortened life expectancy. "They'll discover it for them-selves soon enough," she explained, then added, "I'd like for us to go away for awhile, George. We've been promising ourselves a vacation, but we keep putting it off. Now's the time, Dear."

And so, George and Martha left for three weeks, praised by their grown children for being sensible and good to themselves.

It was when they returned from their vacation and walked from their flight into Boston International Airport that a strange event happened. Martha whispered to George that she wanted to freshen up in the ladies' restroom and left him to wait for a few minutes in the passenger seating area of their airline.

It was just as Martha began her return trip to George from across the wide passenger walkway, that a small, rather timid man with a pale face and a kind, friendly expression stepped up to George and said, "Pardon me, sir, but I have a message for your wife. Do you mind if I give it to her personally? I see her coming across the way."

George briefly inspected the inoffensive little man who stood in front of him. He was slender, dressed in a dark suit and a white shirt with a small, neat tie. His face was pleasant and topped with ginger hair. He certainly did not appear to offer any kind of threat. Oddly, George would remember later that he felt no sense of curiosity about the message for his wife or the messenger.

The stranger intercepted Martha as she approached her husband, and said to her courteously, "Martha, I have an important message for you. You must believe it. You are going to be perfectly all right. There is nothing for you to worry about. You are fine and nothing is going to happen to you."

Before Martha could comment or ask the stranger who he was, he smiled at her, gave her a farewell salute with his right hand, and briskly walked away, soon swallowed in a crowd of passengers.

Of course, Martha told George about the little man's urgent declaration, and during their taxi ride from the airport to their home they discussed and pondered the meaning of the stranger's visit. In her secret heart, Martha had been deeply moved by the messenger's sincerity, the absolute conviction in his voice that she was going to be perfectly all right. She wondered, then decided with rising hope and with a strange certainty that the messenger's firm affirmation was a direct, indisputable reference to her state of health.

When the couple arrived home and collected their phone messages, Martha and George were overwhelmed with excitement by the voice of Dr. Claude Burger:

"Martha, call me at home as soon as you get back. I've got good news for you. My number is … "

The news from Martha's physician was like a burst of sunlight in a room darkened with hopelessness. Instead of a metastasized cancer on her right shoulder, which had been confirmed by five radiologists, the cancer was a rare variety that on film and under a microscope bore a striking resemblance to the more deadly and terminal disease diagnosed by the radiologists.

Martha's physician, struggling to accept the death verdict he had pronounced on his patient, had sent a set of the x-rays with the terminal diagnosis, to an oncologist in San Francisco. While George and Martha were on their vacation, the oncologist had called Dr. Burger. "I'm delighted to tell you boys that your diagnosis is in error. I hope you haven't notified the patient of your findings."

In the telephone conversation Dr. Burger had with Martha to tell her his good news, he informed her that a simple operation of a few minutes to excise the cancer from her back was all that stood between her and excellent health. He would schedule it immediately.

Withdrawn from her death sentence, Martha and her husband looked at one another in awe as they remembered the small, slender messenger at the Boise airport who had promised Martha that she was all right. How did he know? Who was he? Where had he come from?

"How did he know my name?" Martha asked.

It was finally her secret conclusion that she had been visited by an angel. He had been sent from God to relieve her burden, to give her the good news. It was not until many years later that Martha confided the strange and miraculous story to her grown daughter.

I love stories such as the one I've just related. And there are many of them that seem to have a principle message all of us should heed: God sends constant reminders, in the form of angels and little miracles, that life doesn't end with death.

That is the singular purpose of this book, to tell you about my experiences as a grief counselor and to relate some of the remarkable stories of hope, courage and faith I have encountered from people facing death and from those who are learning to say good-bye.

I'll never forget the young woman in her late teens who had become totally blind before her final days on earth. She was a devout Christian and loved statues of figures from the Scriptures. What amazed visitors who came to see her and brought her miniature replicas of saints like Peter, Paul, Luke and John was her uncanny identification of the statues. Though she never once touched or fondled them, she focused her blind eyes on their tiny figures and confidently named them. Even when some visitors, suspecting a trick, silently moved the statues, she was unperturbed and unfailingly reoriented her gaze, gave them their names and said a prayer. She soon passed on into the white light of God.

As you will discover, I came to grief counseling after many experiences with the dead and dying. In retrospect, those happenings were like a trial period in my life, a training for an apprenticeship in the mystery of life and death.

Chapter 2

Great-Grandma Lily

On January 17, 1947 I entered the earthplane. My new family would be my mother, Mary, my father, Philip, and a four-year-old brother, Anthony. Four years later, my sister Connie was born. Next came my sister Carol. We were raised in an apartment in Brooklyn, New York, in a predominantly Italian–Catholic neighborhood. We were close-knit, spending a lot of time with my mother's parents who lived near our home in a three-story building. The first level of the building was my grandparents' furniture store. On the second floor resided my great grandmother, and on the third was my grandparents' apartment.

Great-Grandma Lily, who was born in Italy, was a very soft lady, with snowy white hair and twinkling blue eyes. I clearly remember the day when she passed away. My mother broke into tears when her brother, John, came with the news that Great-Grandma Lily was dead. That was the first time I heard the word death. I was eight years old at the time, and I remember hearing the word "died" without understanding and I became frightened. I had never seen my mother cry and her weeping only heightened my fear of the unknown.

Since we children were told that Great-Grandmother Lily had gone to heaven and would not return, we learned that death meant you just disappeared and were forgotten.

One Sunday, several years after Great-Grandma Lily died, our family visited my grandparents. I was sent by Grandma Concetta to get milk for the coffee always served after dinner. I did not hesitate for a moment, since I was always happy to go into Grecco's Bakery, especially if the baker's daughter, Rosie, was there.

When her parents were absent, Rosie always gave me two cookies — one to eat immediately and one to go on. On good days, Rosie gave me rainbow cookies. The wonderful, sweet smells from the fresh breads, cookies and cakes were always tantalizing.

Rosie and her mother were the only people in our neighborhood who still called me by my real name, Nunzio. I didn't mind them using my legal name, but I refused to answer anybody else who addressed me that way. No one else called me Nunzio. By the first grade, I had decided I would be called Ed.

I was so happy to see Rosie behind the counter and asked her for a quart of milk. Along with the milk she handed me two rainbow cookies.

Pleased by Rosie's gift of two cookies and her parting warning, "And Nunnie, don't put the other one in your pocket, it will get squashed," I ran home and headed up the stairs. Quarter of the way up, I saw Great-Grandma Lily standing on the first floor landing.

As she stood there smiling, hands folded in front of her, my first thought was to go over and kiss her. Then, I remembered to be afraid. My parents had told me that she had gone to heaven. I stood frozen on the stairs just staring up at her smiling face. As always, she wore a flowered, one-piece dress. Her white hair, like a snowy cap, was drawn back in a bun behind her neck.

Cautiously, I crept up the stairs, pressing my back against the railing. When I reached the first floor landing, Great-Grandma Lily was still smiling as I slipped past her. When I had covered half the distance up, I bolted and raced to the top floor. I was so frightened that by the time I clattered to my grandparents' door, I had caused such a commotion that my grandfather rushed into the hallway and started yelling at me. I don't think he paid any attention to my question, "If Great-Grandma's in heaven, why is she on the landing downstairs?"

Ignored by my family, I was easily distracted from my fright by the sweets on the table.

Little did I know that I would see Great-Grandma Lily on the stairway many times in the years to come.

I remembered her custom of stepping out into the hallway to greet all incoming friends and family. But her habit took on a new meaning after her death. To me, when she appeared, it was a warning that somebody in the family would soon die.

Within a week from the first time I saw Great-Grandma standing on the landing, my father died.

Chapter 3

The Wish

As a child I had a speech impediment, which most people call a lisp. My father often teased me about it. He thought that by teasing me, I would realize what I was doing, and correct "a lazy way of speaking."

The last time my father teased me was June 11, 1960. I was thirteen and it was Saturday evening. I felt his treatment was so unjust that I ran to my bedroom and wished him dead. I prayed that I would not have to endure his cruelty ever again.

I thought my prayer was answered, because there was no teasing from my father for the next four days. I had forgotten about wishing for his death, until the morning of June 16. My mother was in the kitchen preparing our lunch. I could hear my father calling us for school, since it was eight o'clock. Like most children, we dreaded getting out of bed on school days. He called our names again from the living room. On his second call, I was out of bed. I heard my mother walk into the living room from the kitchen, calling out my father's name with sudden fear in her voice.

My brother Anthony and I ran into the living room and saw our father slumped over the couch. My mother instructed Anthony to lift and carry him to the window for some air. He rested my father's limp body on a recliner in the dining room near the window. My father called out,

"Mary...." and gasped a final breath.

My mother was frantic. Anthony told me to go down-stairs to the butcher and call for an ambulance. We had no telephone.

Two policemen arrived before the ambulance came. They were very kind to us all. They asked me to call other family members to come to be with my mother. It was forty-five minutes later when the ambulance finally arrived and the paramedics pronounced my father dead of a massive heart attack.

The paramedics covered my father's body with a sheet. I went into my bedroom and told myself, "If I go back to sleep, I will wake up and find out this is only a dream."

As I lay on my bed, I remembered how I'd wished for my father's death. But at that terrible moment I realized I did not want my father to die; in fact, I did not know what death really meant. I would learn about it in the next five days.

My mother insisted on seeing the funeral director take my father's body away. I did not understand where they were taking him. Peering out my bedroom window I saw two men carrying a long, black bag and watched my mother crying uncontrollably.

The limousine arrived on schedule that evening. My immediate family stepped into the elongated car and we drove only a few blocks when we came to a halt in front of Aievoli Funeral Home.

We were helped out of the limousine by the same two men who had carried my father from the house. As we climbed the stairway to the funeral home, two large glass doors were held open for us and my mother started to cry again. In the hallway was a black velvet board with my father's name posted, along with the date, the name of our church, and the place of his burial; Pinelawn National Cemetery, Chapel A. A second set of doors opened for us as if we were going to make a grand entrance. I still did not understand what was happening. Was my father playing a joke?

The doors opened into the largest room I'd ever seen, lined with rows and rows of chairs. The walls were blanketed by large floral arrangements.

My mother let out the most piercing cry I had ever heard. As the men who walked ahead of us stepped aside, I finally saw the reason for my mother's scream: It was my father, laid out stiffly in his coffin. Then, whimpering, my mother leaned over and kissed him.

To me, my father, lying in what I believed was a large jewelry box, looked, somehow, like a young boy at rest, not a man of forty.

My father had blue-black hair. Would I ever see his large charcoal eyes again? Even though my dad was only four feet eleven inches tall, to me he was a giant.

Now, death was starting to have meaning to me.

He was dressed in a black suit, a white shirt and tie, and held rosary beads in his clasped hands. The cross, attached to the rosary, was standing straight up, between his index and forefingers. His hands rested on a small black Bible. On the right of the casket, placed by his feet, there was a floral arrangement shaped like a heart of roses with a banner on which gold script spelled out, "Our Beloved Daddy."

The lid of the casket was cream colored velvet, and attached to it was a large rosary, composed of the tiniest red roses, fifty-three in all. I knew the number because I counted them. Across this rosary was another ribbon which read, "Our Beloved Daddy."

In the corner, on the left side of the casket just above my father's head, was an American flag folded in the shape of a triangle. By the head of the casket stood an enormous heart of roses, with the script, "My Beloved Husband."

It seemed I stood at the casket for the longest time, yet it was only minutes before I ran from the room crying into the arms of my Uncle John, who held me.

Even though I did not understand the meaning of death, as I shed tears I realized that my terrible, terrible wish for my father's death would cause me guilt for many years.

By 6:30 that evening the rows of chairs were all occupied, and there was standing room only as a line of people filed by the casket. As they knelt by my father's coffin, tears flowed, which seemed to bring on a chain reaction from my mother and many others in the room.

At ten o'clock, there was a musical chime from a large grandfather clock, a gentle reminder that it was time to leave. All the mourners once again went up to the casket, knelt down, then walked over to my mother and kissed her good-night; as each person kissed her, she wept.

When it was our turn to visit the casket, my mother stopped sobbing, and once again, kissed my father on the lips. I could hear her say to him, "I will only get to see you for four more days."

On Sunday, it was Father's Day. I bought a small, gold-colored cross for twenty-five cents to pin on my father's lapel, as my last present to him. I also deposited my rosary beads from my First Holy Communion in the coffin with him.

I bent over and whispered, "Happy Father's Day, Daddy."

When my lips touched his forehead, I was shocked by the coldness of his skin.

On the fifth and final day of his public viewing, when we arrived at the funeral parlor for our final good-bye almost every chair was taken. Seated in the front row with my family, I watched my father's stomach to see if he would take a breath or move in any way. I wondered what I would do if his chest did move.

At nine o'clock in the morning, the grandfather clock chimed to tell us that our final visit was coming to a close. Then seven men dressed in black stepped into the room and waited as family and friends made their last farewell. The visitors were ushered out of the room by one of the men in black, and then it was my turn. Quaking and tearful, I whispered into my father's ear that I was sorry for my wish. For the last time, I kissed his forehead and that same cold feeling swept through my body.

Later, the entire funeral procession arrived at Saint Athanasius Church. In the sunlight I noticed the casket had a brassy gold tone and the ornaments on the four corners were gold.

From the moment we got out of the limousine, my mother began sobbing. Pallbearers lifted the casket and placed it on their shoulders. As the casket and pall bearers entered the church courtyard, the doors swung open, awaiting the arrival of my father. It was as if God, with his own two hands, had opened the doors.

I do not recall the mass, but I remember the priest circling the casket and the smell of the incense he carried. I also remember that there were wet marks on the casket from the holy water the priest had used to bless the casket as it went into the church.

When the mass was over, we followed the casket out of the church. We drove toward Long Island, and eventually turned into the gates of Pinelawn Cemetery and drove in until, one by one, all the cars came to a slow stop. We were escorted to the burial site and seated on small white folding chairs. The casket was draped with the American flag. Seven soldiers and a bugler stood in the distance.

The priest began the ceremony. Afterward, there was a seven-gun salute and the bugler played Taps. The American flag was removed from the lid of the casket, folded and presented to my mother. Her tears were uncontrollable at this point. For the final farewell, my mother, Anthony and I were each given a rose and escorted to the casket and told to place the rose on the lid.

My mother was first, standing beside her was her brother, John. She lay down her rose, kissed the casket, and was escorted away. When it was my turn, I placed the rose on the casket and said, "Daddy, I'm sorry."

As I looked down, there was a small opening and I could see into the bottom of the grave. Immediately a fear of being placed in the ground and the worms eating me overtook me. I started weeping and was escorted away. As our car pulled away from the grave, I could see my father's casket being lowered into the ground. It would take me several years before I realized that many children wish for a parent's death.

Later that evening we drove to my grandparents' home. I never again saw the apartment we had lived in before my father's death.

We stayed with my grandparents for about four weeks. By July 15th we moved into a new apartment a few doors away from my grandparents. I did not care about missing my friends. I confined myself to the apartment, except for going to church to pray for forgiveness for the fatal wish that burdened me. When the new school year started, of course, I went to school daily. But at the end of the day, while the other children were outside playing, I stayed inside our apartment.

Chapter 4

The Phone Call

A little more than a month after my father's death in the third weekend of July, the phone rang and my sister, Connie, who was nine, picked it up. I heard her say, "Hello."

Within seconds she was screaming hysterically and my mother and I ran to her while the phone receiver dangled from the wall. I picked it up to see if someone was on the other end, but all I heard was silence.

I replaced the phone on the receiver, while Connie screamed hysterically and repeated, "Daddy, called, Daddy called."

"You know Daddy's not here any longer," my mother admonished.

"No, Daddy called and said, 'Hi Connie, this is Daddy. I just arrived, tell Mommy I am waiting at the airport.'"

It was several months before Connie could pick up the telephone after this incident.

As Christmas neared there was talk of our Christmas tree. My mother thought that a Christmas tree was inappropriate, yet felt that it was unfair to her children not to decorate for the holiday. We made it through Christmas with a tree and gifts on Christmas morning.

Somehow, the family weathered the period of mourning and we got used to living without a strong male presence. One evening — I guess when I was about fifteen — my mother asked me if I would stay with my sisters while she visited my grandparents. Around 9:30, I was sitting on the couch in the living room of our apartment. The windows were opened since it was extremely hot and the kitchen fan did not seem to be stirring up a breeze.

My sisters were asleep in their bedroom located just off the kitchen. I decided that an ice pop would be a cooling treat and I got up to walk toward the refrigerator. There, suddenly, standing directly in front of me was the image of my father. He was moving towards my sisters' room. I became so frightened that I was rooted to the floor.

A few seconds later, when I came to my senses and convinced myself that I was just imagining the vision, I ran to my sisters' room to make sure they were both okay. I noticed the air had a strange chill and realized that our dog was barking frantically and backing away from the bedroom door. When I opened the door, the dog edged even further away and kept on frantically barking.

In the far end of my sisters' bedroom their night light glowed dimly. I reached for the switch on the wall and turned on the overhead light. Carol's pillow was on the floor. I walked over to her side of the bed, picked it up and placed it back under her head. The girls were sound asleep.

Everything in the room seemed to be normal except for the strange chill. The pale pink walls almost appeared to be white. The picture of Jesus, a gift from a friend, seemed to give off a comforting warm glow. I looked over towards Connie's side of the bed; she was fast asleep.

As I turned to leave the room I noticed that their closet door was open. Then I knew I had not imagined my father's presence. The flag which had been draped over his casket was now folded military style, on the floor outside the closet door.

Leaving my sisters' room I did not realize how upset I was over the flag and the whole incident. At the same time my mother returned home and noticing my strange expression, said, "Ed, what is the matter, what happened?"

As I started to speak, with tears running down my face, I told her everything that had taken place. She looked at me in confusion. "Ed, you just imagined this."

"I did not imagine anything," I said. "How did the flag get outside of the closet on the floor?"

She walked into my sisters' bedroom, and just as I had told her, there was the flag lying on the floor.

"Ed, it must have fallen out of the closet."

It was a weak explanation for an event neither of us could explain. After this incident, whenever my father made his presence known to me, the flag somehow appeared.

Chapter 5

The Fan

By the age of fourteen I had become aware of unusual things taking place in my life: visions of events that would take place in the near future and dreams of things to come became part of my everyday life.

One afternoon I went to have lunch with my grandparents. As I entered the building, I noticed Great-Grandma Lily standing at the top of the stairs. This was the second time I had seen her since her passing. An eerie, uneasy feeling came over me making me feel weak in my knees. As I climbed the stairs I said a silent prayer. At this point, I still had not made the connection with the deeper meaning of my great-grandmother's appearances. It was soon to be made clear.

When I arrived at the top of the landing, I continued up the next flight of stairs to my grandparents' apartment. My grandmother was awaiting my arrival and had lunch prepared.

I never mentioned seeing Great-Grandma Lily at the top of the stairs to my grandparents or any of my family, because the first time I described her visit, I had been ignored. After lunch I went home.

That same night, I awoke from a dream so real that I could not shake it. I saw my Uncle Charlie telling silly jokes, as he always did. Suddenly, he grabbed at his chest in pain and fell to the floor. I could see him lying on the floor motionless. I awoke and went into my mother's room and told her about my dream.

"Uncle Charlie died in my dream," I told her.

"It was only a nightmare," she assured me.

Being Italian, with all our superstitions, dreaming of someone's death was actually supposed to mean long life. Later that morning, a black bird flew into the kitchen window. Mom did not get upset often, and when she did she usually hid her emotions from us. Yet, when the bird flew into the house, she acted frightened.

After we chased the bird out through an open window, Rose, our neighbor from the floor below, opened the door to see what was happening and heard about the bird from us. She did not look at me but directly at my mother and said, "Mary, do you know what that means?"

"No, no. I don't," my mother said sharply. It was almost as if she did not want me to hear Rose's explanation.

Oblivious of my mother's nervousness, Rose said, "The black bird is a sign that someone's going to die."

My mother looked at me, then back at Rose, and again at me. Just then the phone rang. One of our relatives was on the phone delivering the unhappy news that Uncle Charlie had passed away.

After this incident I became more aware that I had the strange ability to see and hear things that none of my other friends ever spoke of. For example, a few months later my youngest sister, Carol, was invited to go swimming with one of her playmates and her mother. I asked my mom, "Where is Carol? I haven't seen her around?

"She went swimming with Lidia."

Immediately, I pressed her, "Why did you let her go?"

"She has adult supervision," Mom answered.

"She is going to get hurt," I warned my mother.

"Why do you have to say things like that, Ed?"

"Mom, she is going to get hurt," I insisted. No sooner had I expressed my alarm, than the doorbell rang. It was one of the other parents coming to tell my mother that Carol needed stitches in her head.

Once again, I had been given an insight about something before it happened.

My family, of course, thought it was strange when I forecast the future. Usually they just looked at me and shrugged it off. I did not know that my mother's secret fear was the paranormal and that many years earlier my father had a visit from the angelic realm when he was twenty-one. He was told that he would die by his fortieth birthday.

Within a week of Carol's injury, a bowl filled with gravy and meatballs fell in the kitchen. As I went to help clean up the mess, Carol started towards the kitchen. I advised her not to go into the kitchen. She would be hurt and this time it would be more serious than a few stitches.

No sooner had I uttered the warning, than Carol, heedless of my prediction, slipped across the kitchen floor and almost lost three fingers. As she looked down at her fingers hanging by mere threads of skin, she accused me: "You did this." And then she burst into tears.

Once again, Carol was taken to the hospital.

My clairvoyance, unfortunately, seemed to be targeted at Carol. The next incident again involved her and a broken glass door. Once again, she required stitches. On this occasion, when Mom and Carol arrived home from the hospital we were in the kitchen. I asked Carol, "What happened in the hallway?"

She insisted that she slipped and her fist went through a glass pane. I knew she was not telling the truth.

"Why are you always picking on her?" my mother asked.

"She is not telling you the truth," I answered. "She purposely put her hand through the glass."

As I started to tell my mother exactly what took place, Carol said, "You weren't there, you weren't even home when this happened. How would you know?"

"Why are you making up a story?" my mother demanded of me. "You're lying."

"Mom," I said, "I'm going to prove it to you. I'm not lying, Carol is."

I pointed at the kitchen fan which sat on the window sill; it had an on and off switch.

"Mom, do you see the fan in the window?"

"Of course, I see the fan in the window," Mom answered.

"Well, I'm going to turn it on, and that's how I'm going to prove to you that I'm telling the truth."

"I can go over and turn on the fan, too," Carol said.

"No, I am going to turn the fan on from here," I answered.

I was ten feet from the fan and angry that my mother did not believe me, so I pointed my right arm as if it were fueled anger in the direction of the fan switch, and the fan went on.

All of us, including me, stared at the fan in amazement. My mother's first conclusion was that the fan had an on and off thermostat. Then she suggested that the wind was so strong that it turned the fan on.

At that point, Carol became frightened and told the truth. She had put her fist through the glass.

"Why would you do something like this?" my mother asked her.

"For attention," Carol replied.

I was amazed that the fan actually turned on. I did not understand that a person's energy could move an object.

To this day I have never attempted or tried to use this type of energy again.

Chapter 6

Heaven is Like a Garden

I was sixteen years old, without a care. Once again, school was out. My two sisters and my mother were vacationing in Florida for four weeks. Anthony was married and living ten minutes away. I liked the idea of being almost alone, of taking care of myself.

There was plenty of food, since my grandparents lived just a few doors away. Grandma was an excellent cook, but Grandpa was a better chef. I spent time shuffling back and forth to their apartment collecting my dinner and pocket change. On occasion, a friend would stay over. On Saturday, the third weekend in July, it seemed that no one was around.

I realized my family would be home from Florida soon and it would take me at least a week to get the apartment back in order. I started gathering the dirty glasses and the dishes scattered throughout the apartment and decided on a plan of action. If I cleaned up the kitchen today, and the bathroom the next, and so on, the place would be neatly in order twenty-four hours before they returned.

I started with the dishes, got about halfway through and took a break by going into the living room to watch TV. Before I knew it, the afternoon had slipped away. I realized that I had never finished the dishes and it was already night time. Then without warning, Mitzie, our dog, began barking. I started toward her and noticed that she was barking at nothing, but was looking intensely in the direction of my sister's room. I opened her bedroom door and, once again, I felt that strange chill in the air, which I knew signaled my father's presence.

I quickly decided that before fear overcame me I would investigate the room. I tried to coax Mitzie to go into the room first, but she stopped at the doorway and kept barking.

I got her leash, attached it to her collar, and tried to drag her in, but she kept on pulling back and would not go into the bedroom. I finally succeeded in dragging her into the bedroom with me, and saw that one of the drawers of the dresser was open and the American flag was lying in that drawer.

I do not recall taking the dog's leash off, shutting off the lights, or locking the door. The ten-minute distance to my brother's house took me less than five. When I arrived I was shaken, and that evening I slept at Anthony's house. However, by the next day, it was almost as if the incident never happened.

I decided it would be best to go home, take care of the dog, and get the apartment together. However, I never went back into my sister's room to see if the flag was still there.

The next summer, during the third weekend in July, I once again felt my father's vibration. I hurried to my brother's home once again. On my way I saw my grandmother on the avenue with some neighborhood women taking fresh air. I told her the story and she suggested that I speak to a priest.

The next day, I went to my parish and asked to speak to a priest. I met with Father Mac. When I told him about my visions, and my father's visits from the "other side," he advised me to pray.

"You have to pray," Father Mac told me. "And get those evil thoughts out of your mind. Only God can tell the future. And as far as your father is concerned, this is where your blood runs cold like a vampire, and it is why you need prayer."

I looked at him in disbelief, but reasoned that he knew more than I did since he was closer to God and had more answers.

"What do you mean about my blood running cold? I don't understand."

"Your thoughts are evil," he replied. "And you must pray."

I was even more confused. Why was I evil because I had the ability to communicate with the "other side" and had premonitions? I had not lost my love for God, nor the church, but I was upset and angry with a superstitious priest for calling me evil and comparing me to a vampire. I knew it would take me a long time to remove the sting of his words from my memory.

I've come to believe that people who possess a gift like mine truly carry a cross. There have been many times throughout the years when I believed there was something wrong with me. But each new lesson I learned and each communication from the other side helped me to expand my awareness and granted me the confidence to give those around me comfort and joy.

About two years later, once again during the third week in July, Mom was vacationing in Florida with my sister Carol, while Connie stayed with my Aunt Rosalie on Long Island. I was never fearful of staying home except during this period of time.

It was Saturday, and without mentioning my uneasiness, I asked my girlfriend, Lois, if she would help me clean the apartment before Mom returned home. She agreed to help me. Since it was such a hot day we decided to go to the beach first. After the beach and dinner we returned to clean the apartment. It was not in such bad shape this time. We started in my bedroom, next cleaned the living room, dusted the dining room, and finally worked in the kitchen.

I decided I should sweep the hallway stairs, while Lois was finishing in the kitchen. As I stood in the hallway with the broom I could hear Mitzie barking. Lois called out to me and I came back into the apartment. She asked me, "Why is the dog barking at your sister's bedroom door?"

At this time in our relationship, I did not wish to share my past experiences with Lois. I thought that if I told her about my clairvoyance she would think that I was out of my mind. But I knew I had to open the door and look in the bedroom. When I opened the door, Lois, who followed me in, asked where the cold air was coming from.

I did not bother to look around for the flag, I knew it would be visible somewhere. Suddenly, the mop slammed to the floor and Lois screamed, "I want to go home."

She claimed that she felt spooked, and of course, I had not given her an explanation for the cold air or the mop that moved on its own. Once again, I quickly left the apartment, accompanied by Lois.

I walked her home and continued on to Anthony's, where I found his wife, Vicki, and told her about my experience at the apartment.

Vicki tried to assure me that it was mind over matter and I should not worry about the strange happenings. While she spoke I could see her looking at my hands curiously. She asked me why my hands were so red. I looked at my hands, then at my feet and noticed they were bright red. I remembered that a few days earlier I had prayed for peace of mind, asking God if he would give me a sign with my hands and feet, so that I would not be afraid of my father's untimely visits. Vicki continued to look at me strangely, and as I explained my prayer, the redness in my skin subsided as quickly as it appeared.

Later, when Anthony came home, he flung open the door and announced, "I've never felt such an eerie feeling before, I felt like there was someone following me up the stairway."

At this time, Anthony did not know what had taken place at my mother's house, or that I was in his kitchen. That's when I told him about my sister's room and Vicki chimed in about my hands and feet. He described in more detail the sensations he felt in the hallway, a definite coldness that frightened him, then he asked me for Lois' number to verify my story.

Later after dinner, Vicki went to get the sheets for the couch to make up my "fright-night" sleeping quarters, and I told my brother that he was sleeping with me.

We took our positions in the living room on the pull-out bed. After talking for about fifteen minutes, Anthony said he was really tired and got up to shut off the light. I wanted to ask him to leave the light on, but I did not. I thought if he was giving up his own bed to keep me company, how could I force him to leave the light on?

About ten minutes later, I felt a presence in the room. Anthony was sound asleep. As the presence moved toward me, I could not utter a word, I was so frightened. As the image began to speak, the voice was familiar. The sound of it was like an angel's harp, soothing every part of my being.

"What do you want from me?" I asked. "You frighten me."

"I truly love you and I came to say I am sorry," the voice answered. "I didn't mean to frighten you. When I walked on earth there were lessons I had to learn. Again, I did not mean to cause you pain."

"I will listen to all you have to say," I answered. "But you have to make a promise. After tonight you will never come to visit me again because I'm afraid of you."

I asked a question of the voice before it could reply to my previous statement.

"Is there a heaven?" I asked. "And what is heaven like?"

The reply was, "You should not fear death, it is only a transition, a process that is needed."

"Why?" I asked.

"There are some things I cannot tell you, you will learn them in time."

"But what is heaven?" I persisted.

"Heaven is like a garden of the most beautiful flowers, filled with tranquility, peace and total love."

"There are things I need to tell you," the voice said. "Tell your mother that she should start being happy. I am only a breath away. You are truly the head of the household."

"That's not so," I protested. "My brother is older so that makes him head of the household."

"No, you have the strength to carry many burdens. You may not understand this strength at this moment, but you will. Your sister-in-law carries a child. When your first child comes, he will be named after me."

I needed to be certain who the voice belonged to so I asked, "What is your name?"

There was no reply. "Your sister, Carol, will go through difficult times. Connie, one day, will become like your mother."

I said, "I am going to be getting married next year. Will this be a happy, good marriage?"

"This you must learn for yourself. Tell your mother I love her very dearly. Do not become frightened with what I'm about to tell you. One day all her worldly possessions will burn."

"Is my mother going to die in a fire," I asked. "Is this what you're telling me?"

"Do not fear, for no one will be hurt. My time is short and I have to go."

"Why?"

"We are only allowed to spend so much time here," the voice replied.

"Before you go I have to remind you to remember your promise not to come and visit me anymore."

"I will not break that promise. I'm only a breath away."

"What shall I call you?" I asked.

"As you've always called me. 'Daddy.' "

As the voice said those last words I felt peace within. I lost all fear of dying. In fact, I believed that death was not to be feared, it was to be embraced. I did not realize that my father was the beginning of the work that I would be doing someday.

I woke up Anthony and told him everything I had heard.

The next morning, I told Vicki that she was going to have a baby.

"I did not think you were nuts last night," she said. "But I do now because I'm not pregnant."

Eight months later the baby was born. It was a little girl, Tiffany. I knew then my first-born would be a boy and we would name him Philip — after my father.

I did not understand why my father came to me the third weekend in July since it was not the anniversary of his death. There would be another major event nineteen years later during the month of July, of which I had no inkling at the time.

Chapter 7

Good and Bad

We go through life receiving many daily signs. The night before my first wedding, I was running errands when someone closed a car door on my left ring finger. If this happened to me today, and there was a marriage taking place tomorrow, I would stop to consider what the message from the Universe meant.

Later, when my wife and I exchanged wedding rings, my ring would not fit because my finger was swollen. Even while I was standing at the altar watching Lois, my wife-to-be, come down the aisle, my inner voice said to me, "You shouldn't marry this girl, this marriage will only last six months. She's only marrying you to get away from her step-father."

As it turned out, the marriage was one of many painful lessons in my life. Five months after the wedding, I asked Lois if she were seeing someone else. She denied there was anyone else in her life, but a month later she admitted to having an affair with a co-worker during her lunch hour.

We were divorced on May 4, 1969 and that evening I met a petite, beautiful blonde girl, with the most magnificent blue eyes. Her name was Prudence. I took one look at her and told my friend, Richie, "You see that girl there? I'm going to marry her."

"How could you marry her, you don't even know her."

"Richie, just look at her. She looks like an angel."

We were married on March 1, 1970, and my best man, Richie, was at my side.

Nine months later on December 22, a special event took place in which I dreamed about my Aunt Frances, who had died of cancer. She appeared to me, looking healthy and happy, yet during the interval of the dream she was engaged in pulling yarn. Long skeins of yarn flowed through her fingers. It seemed as if the strands were never ending, since she kept pulling and pulling. The strands were very thick, like a tube, and fastened to the tube was a baby-blue bow. Attached to the end of the tube was a beautiful baby boy.

The next morning my wife's parents and I rushed my pregnant wife to the hospital. We learned from the doctor that there were complications. The baby would have to be taken by caesarean.

I prayed to Saint Joseph that my wife and child would be safe. Later that evening, we went back to visit her and discovered that her labor had stopped. It started again much later, and at about 8:15 the next morning, I felt severe pain in my lower abdomen, as if I had been kicked in the groin. I rushed to the bathroom, trying to expel the pain. When, finally, I was able to release it, I began to sweat. That was when I knew, as I later told my mother-in-law, that Prudence was giving birth.

On our way to the hospital, I remembered my dream about Aunt Frances. I realized that the never-ending roll of yarn she kept pulling with her hands represented my wife's extended labor. And the baby that appeared in the same dream was a dead ringer for my new son, Philip, who was born later that day.

Also, I remembered with a sense of awe the last visit from my father many years earlier when he told me that I would have a son and I would name him Philip.

Chapter 8

Green Tea Room

At the time of Philip's birth, I was working as a buyer in May's Department Store. There was a stock boy named Carlos, with whom I became friendly. Whenever Carlos decided to get in touch with me, he sent telepathic messages. I did not know what was happening, until the day I was on the fifth floor and Carlos was in the basement stockroom. Carlos' name kept popping into my mind, and, as much as I tried to concentrate on what I was doing, I could not get it out of my thoughts. I picked up the telephone and called the stockroom where Carlos answered and said,

"Hi, it's Ed."

When Carlos heard my voice he started laughing. "It works, it works," he said.

"What works Carlos?"

"I wanted you to call me," he said. "So I just kept

thinking of your name over and over; and here you are."

Carlos's admission led me to confide in him that I had been given power to see into the past and the future. I was surprised at my confession, for I seldom spoke to anyone about my clairvoyant abilities.

He said I was indeed gifted, but afraid of what I could not understand.

He recommended that I visit a woman in Manhattan at the Green Tea Room, but my first instinct was to ignore his suggestion. Then, he held out his hand, palm up, and asked me to tell him about his life. As I examined his palm, I could hear words flowing from my lips, as if I could not stop myself from speaking, describing who he was by virtue of a wisdom that came from me like a hidden spring breaking free.

I had never studied palmistry, but I knew in my inner being that the information I was giving Carlos was accurate. I felt comfortable with the predictions I was making, and Carlos confirmed that everything I told him was accurate.

He repeated his suggestion that I visit the Green Tea Room. Resistance to the idea that I visit a psychic reader came from Prudence. She did not want me to go, insisting that psychics were gypsies, and they were somehow dangerous.

I thought it best not to argue the point. Whether the psychic was a gypsy or not, I was going. I did promise to call Prudence from the city when the reading was finished.

The psychic I met was named Betsy. I was fascinated with her beautiful smile and intense brown eyes.

"Can I help you?" she asked.

"Yes," I said. "I came for a reading."

She looked directly into my eyes, and I never will forget what she said.

"Why would *you* come here for a reading?"

Her question confused me until she added quickly, "Young man, you are highly gifted."

I just stood there staring at her in surprise. "Well, in any case," I insisted. "I would still like a reading."

The statement I remember most from her reading was when she said, "You hold the keys to the universe. You have a natural gift, or should I say, gifts of psychic, telepathic, audio clairvoyance, and psychometry. You were born with these innate abilities. "Then with her eyes burning directly into mine, as if she were trying to pierce my soul, Betsy said, "You have spoken to many people who have passed over."

"What do you mean?" I asked, feeling trapped.

For a moment, she remained silent, slipping into a trance state, then she said, "I am told to ask you who was the woman in the hallway?"

I had never told anyone outside my family about my sightings of my great-grandmother. Now I found myself explaining those events to a stranger and how frightened I was.

"Your grandmother was not your only visitor," she said mater-of-factly. "Why did you tell your father not to visit you anymore?"

My eyes welled up with tears. I now trusted Betsy and told her the story of my father's appearances.

"Oh, my dear," she answered, "there will be many visits from many other people's loved ones."

"What do you mean by that?" I asked.

"In time you will understand." Betsy said deviously. Then she added, "As I told you when we first started, you hold the keys to the universe. Always remember your insight is a gift from God."

Many of the things Betsy told me that day confused

and excited me. But her reading allowed me to understand some of the unexplainable things that had taken place in my life. I tried to contact Betsy many times, but she disappeared, never again to work at the Green Tea Room. It was as if she had vanished from the earth.

Chapter 9

Philip and My Father

For the first two years of my marriage to Prudence we lived at 85th Street in Brooklyn with my wife's parents while an apartment in Park Slope, Brooklyn, was being prepared for us.

Only a week after we moved in with my in-laws, I had a dream in which all of our belongings we had stored in the basement were stolen. I woke up from the dream in the middle of the night tempted to check the basement door.

I decided against the idea since I'd have to wake my father-in-law for the key. What if my dream was a false alarm?

As I was leaving for work the next morning, I decided to check the outside entrance to the basement. The door was ajar as I approached. I could see the basement had been invaded; all our belongings were gone!

The loss of clothing, linens, dishes, was not as upsetting to me as losing the cherished keepsakes I had received from my relatives who had passed over; they were priceless. One item missing was an embossed, gold-lettered plaque on which was printed The Lord's Prayer. It had been given to me by Aunt Frances' family after she died. The price tag was still on the back, marked only ninety-nine cents, yet this was a treasure that could never be replaced.

Another cherished item was my father's belt buckle with the initial "P" inscribed on it. I had hoped to give it to my son one day. I believe that when things are taken from us, God also sends us rays of love. The person who took The Lord's Prayer must have needed this message. I imagined the thief or thieves would be surprised to discover that they had stolen the words of God. I hoped that they would read this special prayer every day. Maybe it would change their paths in life.

Shortly after this incident, still not trusting my own insights or dreams, as I was leaving the building, I glanced at my mother-in-law's car and noticed that the front fender looked dented. I walked over to the car and put my hand on the fender. It was perfectly fine, there was not a mark anywhere. Yet the dented fender appeared to me three mornings in a row.

On the fourth morning, I did not even bother to examine the car. As I started up the block to my own car, a neighbor asked, "Did you see your mother-in-law's car?"

I went over to the vehicle and saw at once that the front fender had been damaged during the night.

For the three days when I verified that the car was fine, I had justifiably thought my premonition was a dream, but on the fourth day the smashed fender taught me that the time a vision appears to the beholder and its material manifestation later is proof that delays occur between thought and action. Manifestation of a dream can come to full fruition in days, weeks, or even months later.

Philip was barely three years old when I overheard him talking to someone in the dining room. As I stepped into the room, I saw that he was facing an empty corner and chattering away to someone who was not there. I did not want to interrupt or startle him so when he finished giggling and talking, I asked him, "Philip, who are you speaking to?"

"I am talking to Papa," he said.

"No, Philip, Papa's upstairs." I thought Philip was referring to my wife's father who lived in the apartment above us.

"No, Daddy," he said. "Papa Philip."

My son had never even seen a photograph of my father. The next Sunday we went to visit my mom. I took out a photograph of my father and showed it to my son, and asked who he saw in the photo.

"Daddy," he answered. "That's Papa Philip, who I talk to."

I did not believe that it was right to question him, although I was curious about his conversations. I was afraid that if I questioned him, he would become fearful and possibly close down to the universal messages. I knew then that my young son was able to see the visions that I also saw.

Prudence and I were expecting a new addition to our family. Philip was very excited that he was going to have a baby brother. There was no doubt in his mind, nor mine that we would have a baby boy. Anthony was born on November 8th, 1974.

At this time, our lives were going really well. I had just started a new business, a florist and wedding center. We had enough money saved to put a down payment on a house, and a little left over for a rainy day. Being a Capricorn, I always prepared for rainy days. Philip longed for a yard to play in. He did not like the cement sidewalks of Brooklyn any longer. We started to look for a home in Staten Island. After inspecting several houses, and finding nothing to our liking, once again I had a dream.

I dreamt that I walked into a house with a hallway covered in red paneling. The walls leading up the stairway were covered with the same ugly red paneling. I woke from the dream and thought nothing of it.

However, within a week we went to look at a home that was lovely on the outside. In fact, from the charming exterior, it seemed like it was just what we wanted. Then the realtor opened the door, revealing the ugly red paneling from my dream. Without inspecting any other part of the house, I knew that this was our new home. We moved in January of 1975.

Chapter 10

Signora Maria

After moving into our new home I took a week off from the store. On my return to work, it seemed that it was going to be a slow day, so I decided to catch up on some overdue paperwork. However, I was interrupted when my mother called me into the showroom to meet a little old Italian woman. She was well dressed, with skin as smooth as satin, charcoal eyes, and hair that seemed to be even darker. When she spoke she used broken English with a heavy Italian accent. In one hand, she held a walking stick, in the other, a small gift-wrapped box. My mother introduced her as Signora Maria. As I walked over to greet Maria, she handed me the gift.

"This is for your new home," she said.

I had seen Maria come in and out of my store to buy plants and soil. She would take the merchandise, and within a week or two come in and pay for it and take something else. But for some unknown reason I had always kept my distance from her.

"Signora, how do you know about my new home?" I asked.

"I know lotsa things," she replied.

I thanked her for her gift and told her that I would bring it home for my wife to open.

This was my first conversation with Maria and it puzzled me why I was repelled by her. As I turned around to go back to my paperwork, I heard a thumping on the floor. I turned around and there was Maria who had picked up her walking stick and was thumping it lightly on the floor.

"You will be busy today," she said.

I just smiled at her, then glanced at my mom, shrugged my shoulders, and went back to my paperwork.

It was not more than ten minutes later that the store became so unbearably busy, we needed to call in two part-time employees to help out. By early evening, when we had finally slowed down, I asked my mother if she had told Maria that I bought a house. She said she had never mentioned it to her.

"Do you think there was a connection with her tapping and us getting so busy today?" I asked my mother.

I should have realized the response I would get from such a question. I was ignored. The following day, at a few minutes before 10:00 AM, Maria came into the store, and I thanked her for her lovely music box. Maria, again, began to tap on the floor.

"Caro Mio," she said. "Today you will be busy."

Again, she tapped three more times on the floor. Once more, the customers kept us so busy that I had to call in the two part-time employees.

We did not see Maria until about a week later when she next came into the store. This time, I was standing in the showroom.

"Hello Signora, what can I do for you?" I said.

From the sound of her voice it was obvious that she was just getting over a cold. She asked for potting soil. Hearing her voice, my mother came from the back and started speaking Italian with her, of which I understood very little. Maria was telling my mother that she had been ill for a week and unable to leave her house. Today she was forced to shop because she had nothing in the house to eat.

"Don't you have children that could help you?" my mother asked.

"I wasa not fortunate to hava children," Maria said. "I hava two step-daughters and they no very nice-a to me."

"If you ever need anything," my mother told Maria, "Give us a call and we'll bring it over to you."

This conversation began a weekly ritual for the next several years because from then on, whenever Maria was ill and needed something, she would call me to bring it to her.

Every time Maria came in to the store she would invite us to come to her home for espresso. I always declined her invitation, that is, until April of 1975.

On this day, Maria called the store and said she was not feeling well. She sounded weak on the phone when she asked if I could buy her saltines and milk.

I did not hesitate. I said yes immediately. After which I went to the grocer and bought what she needed, along with a few other grocery items. These I brought to her house. Maria invited me in.

A startling thought occurred to me as I stepped though the door. In fact, my first impression once inside Maria's home was that it was my house.

We went into the kitchen. On the kitchen table were two demitasse cups of espresso and a plate of biscuits. She invited me to sit down, and I did. As I sat there, she looked into my eyes and she began to tell me about my past, as if she were reading from a book. It seemed that Maria had been clairvoyant all of her life.

Maria spoke about a past life I'd lived in Egypt. She told me that on my fiftieth birthday I would be making what she called "a spiritual journey to Egypt."

She mentioned the lisp I had as a child, and the pain it brought to me. She also told me that I should not be afraid of communicating with the "other side." She called these communications "my teachers."

Then she proceeded to tell me what would take place in my future.

By this time I had invested in several real estate properties. She prophesied that I would buy a property that was much taller than the other buildings, and this building would bring many difficulties.

Maria was so accurate about my past history that long after her death her predictions would continue to play out in my future.

She told me that my wife was going to have another baby and this time it would be a girl. She also reaffirmed my gift of insight and the lessons I needed to learn. With this gift, the most important lesson was to allow the information from beyond to flow, not to fear the messages I received. Maria explained that if I held back delivering a message from the universe, I would be holding back the person the message was intended for.

"The people willa come to you like you are a magnet," she predicted.

"Maria, I really don't think so," I protested.

"Someday youa will," she smiled.

From that day on, whenever I was able, I visited with my new friend, Signora Maria.

We got to know each other very well, in fact, she became like one of the family. By this time I was also calling her the Italian Robin Hood. She would call and invite me to come for coffee if I was able to visit with her, if not, she would she would send a tray with a demitasse pot, cups, and biscuits for my mother and me.

Her strategy was that I would be forced to return the demitasse set, thus guaranteeing a visit from me that day. If I tried to return the coffee things with one of my staff, she would send the tray and cups back to the store until I returned everything in person.

One day while returning the tray, I went into her kitchen. As we stood in the kitchen she asked if I could do her a favor.

"Could you go to the butch?"

"Maria, who is the butch?" I asked.

"The butch," she said again.

"And what do I do at the butch?"

"You buya the meat," she replied.

I started laughing so hard, I could see Maria was becoming angry.

"You laugh at mya English," she fumed. "You say it in Italian."

"Dabutch," I answered.

Buying meat for Maria became my new ritual every week. Maria knew I would never take her money. So after our visit, I went to the butcher, ordered meat, and had it delivered to Maria's home. The next day, on my daily visit, I asked her how she enjoyed the meat.

"Caro Mio," she sighed. "You know whata happened?

My friend'a husband leavea her. She crya so hard, I bringa her the meat."

I thought she was teasing me, so I got up and looked in the freezer. It was empty. Of course, I returned to the butcher and placed another order.

It seemed that no matter what Maria asked me to buy for her, she always managed to give it away. It was during the summer when she announced that her washing machine had broken. Little did I know that it had been broken for years, and she did all her laundry by hand. She asked me, "Do you thinka you coulda lend me money and I'll paya you back every week?"

I said, "Maria, what do you need?"

"My washing machinea, she don't work, she broken."

I found myself in the appliance store buying my little old lady-friend a new washing machine. It was a week later when it was delivered to her home.

I was out of town for a week vacationing with my family when the washing machine was delivered. On my return visit I asked Maria how she liked her new appliance. I had discovered that whenever Maria was going to tell me a fib, for some reason she wouldn't use the familiar term of affection, Caro Mio. Instead she would use my name, adding an "H" so that Ed would sound like "Head."

That was my clue that I was going to hear another Robin Hood story.

"The washing machinea," she explained. "She didn't worka so good, she leaka all over my floor, so I sold her."

"Maria, how much did you sell her for?"

"I no sella her, I sella the washing machinea." With that, she smiled.

"Maria," I said. "You speak English better than I do."

"Head, I givea you whata I sold her for."

"Maria, I didn't ask you for the money; how much did you sell the washing machine for?"

"You makea nicea profit," she said. "Fifty dollars."

"Maria, a washing machine costs close to four hundred dollars, and it's not the money. I bought it for you."

"Caro," she went on. "Thesea people so poor."

"Yes, but if you continue doing this, you are going to make me poor," I replied.

"Oh, my Caro, youa never be poor."

I did not consider myself naive, nor did I consider myself foolish, but Maria had a way of getting to my heart, and into my pocket. The washing machine was only one of many items I bought for her without ever receiving payment. Her total income was less than four hundred dollars a month. How could I take money from this wonderful, loving, adorable Robin Hood?

Five years passed and our friendship grew. Maria spent many hours with me and my family. I have never met another person of seventy-seven who had as many friends as she did.

Chapter 11

The Crystal Ball

I decided to take a weekend off from the store. My wife thought it would be nice to visit her aunt who lived in Syracuse, New York. We phoned Aunt Annie and made arrangements for our trip. Aunt Annie was excited, because she had not met any of our children, only knew them from photographs.

When we arrived at her old Victorian mansion, I was stunned by the beautiful antiques that graced her home. There was furniture from all over the world: signed original oil paintings, Louis XIV sofas and chairs, lamps, silver, brass, and rare china. An antique dealer would have had a picnic among all her treasures. I loved to roam around the house and examine all of these wonderful objects.

Aunt Annie's husband, Carl, had passed away ten years earlier and much of the furnishings had belonged to his mother and grandmother. Among the collection were letters from Houdini and President Theodore Roosevelt. I also learned that Carl had been known as the most gifted psychic healer of his time. While he was alive he had two diamonds in his front teeth, which now rested comfortably in a ring on Aunt Annie's finger.

My wife and I slept in the master bedroom with its 1920s wallpaper, and high poster bed, with a matching cherry wood and marble-topped dresser. In the far corner of the room was another marble-topped stand holding an oversized, antique wash basin.

As we got ready to go to bed, I turned off the lights, yet a few seconds later the lights switched back on. Again, I turned off the lights, and again they came back on. My wife was frightened, but I just laughed. Earlier in the day, as Aunt Annie and I were sitting on the front porch, she told me that sometimes she was aware of her husband's presence.

My wife told me she had to go to the bathroom, but she was not going alone. We got out of bed and she put on her slippers. We went to the bathroom, then we came back to the bedroom, where she took off her slippers and left them on her side of the bed. The next morning when she searched for her slippers, they were gone. She made me get up to find them and I discovered that they were now on my side of the bed. Was this Carl's way of making his presence known?

During the night we'd heard footsteps walking back and forth in the attic. Of course, I decided to investigate after breakfast. I climbed the back stairway and was again taken by surprise. Before me stood a life-sized painting of Aunt Annie's husband, Carl Kramer, known for his psychic ability and mystical healing powers. As I looked up at the painting, I was startled, for as I climbed the steps I sensed his eyes burrowing into me. Later, when I asked Aunt Annie about the painting, she explained that it was in the attic stairway because she could no longer bear to have his eyes following her.

I could feel Carl's vibrations within the house, but I did not communicate with him. I was not aware at the time that I could reach into other dimensions to speak with spirits. Instead, I thought that spirits had to contact me.

One day during our visit, as I approached the library, I slowly opened the doors. Directly in front of me was the carved fireplace, to the right was a large, carved wooden chair. Resting across the arms of the chair was a silk robe, and on top of the robe lay a walking stick. I realized that I had not asked permission to enter this room so I left the room and closed the doors behind me.

Later on that day, I asked Aunt Annie if I could go into the library and look around. Smiling, she told me it would be fine. As I re-entered the library, my eyes went to the chair and immediately I noticed that the silk robe was arranged differently, as was the walking stick. I did not become frightened, I became more inquisitive.

To the left of the library was another room. Carl used this room for meditation. In the center of the room was a long, wooden table and two chairs. I noticed a magnificent crystal ball in the center of the table along with the many other mystical treasures. I could hear my inner voice telling me that all I would have to do is ask and the crystal ball could be mine. I no longer feared my inner voice, so I decided to ask Aunt Annie and the crystal ball became one of my prized possessions. Crystal balls have the ability to reflect visionary patterns and are used by those who are able to perceive other dimensions.

My wife was happy when it was time for us to say good-bye, while I could happily have stayed another week examining all of the wonderful treasures in my wife's aunt's "museum."

When we arrived home, I worked with the crystal ball until my eyes hurt. After several weeks, I started to use what is called "soft vision." This is the process by which a person looks at the crystal ball gently, lovingly, his eyes fixed slightly above the top of the ball. There is no strain on one's eyes looking at the ball in this manner. One day, the little air bubbles in the crystal globe started to expand, and then, when my focus permitted me to see only the perimeter of the ball, it became milky white. The milkiness seemed to clear, and there within I saw a woman, holding a walking stick. I could also see a date: August 20. I realized that the vision in the crystal ball was of my friend, Signora Maria. I was surprised at the vision, because I knew that another person I loved and cared for would be leaving earthplane. I put the ball back in its chemise sack. I did not take it out for several years, because after that vision of Maria I could feel fear stir in my stomach. I thought back to my conversation with Father Mac many years before and his foolish, superstitious words, "Your blood runs cold like a vampire."

I was still not ready for the gift of sight.

Chapter 12

Maria's Passing

Toward the end of Maria's life while she was hospitalized only one other visitor besides myself was allowed
at her bedside; my wife, Prudence. Maria was so ill and
spent so much time hospitalized that she was no longer
concerned with her friends' troubles. She stopped asking me
to go to the "butch" and dropped all her antics to help her
needy friends. Sadly, when her generosity ended, all the
people around her withdrew.

The night before Maria's passing, my father-in-law
was in the same hospital and my wife and I went to visit
him. I asked my wife if we could shorten the visit with her
father so that we could also pay a call on Maria.

I remembered my vision of Maria, the one I'd seen in
the crystal ball and the date, August 20. It was now August
19. Even though I was afraid to trust that vision, I knew that
Maria's time was short.

I had told my wife that Maria was not doing well, but I had not given her any details about her condition. When we arrived at the hospital the day Maria died, we entered the Intensive Care Unit, and Prudence looked at me as if I had lied to her about Maria's condition. We were surprised to find Maria sitting up in bed, looking well, chatting away with the nurses. She greeted my wife and me lovingly.

During our conversation she asked me for one last favor, "Caro Mio," she chuckled. "He'sa likea my boyfriend," she explained to my wife.

I knew better than to ask her what she was plotting. She waited a few minutes and then looked into my eyes.

"I must tella you these things so you are prepared," she began. "In the red box, where my tarot cards are, is my will. This is onea thing that I can't givea away, my funeral. In exchangea for my funeral, I leavea you my house. Mya home was yours from the firsta day that I meta you. Even if youa had not donea alla those wonderful thingsa for me. Youa do not have to spenda too mucha money. I have a plot, and I woulda like to be buried with mya husband, Roberto.

"They'll only be eleven people at my funeral," she continued. "And after I'ma with Roberto, most of thesea people will comea to you and tella you that I promised them mya personal things. You don't givea anything to anyone. When I closea my eyes, you aska my boarder to leave. There isa something very special that I have wanted to givea to you for the longest time, make sure youa tell him to leave."

"Maria, don't talk like this," I begged.

"Justa remember everythinga I havea said," she replied. "And looka for the black velvet bag, there are gold coins ina the bag, Roberto gavea them to me as gifts. This is the only money I have."

"Maria, I do not care about the money, or your house,"

I protested.

She interrupted, "Caro, only onea more thing, and it's not too mucha money. I was paying Mr. Gordon fiva dollars a week for mya wrist watch. I still owe him twenty-fiva dollars. And youa know Mr. Campo, ina the gift store. He is honest, he will tell youa exactly how mucha I owe him. I don't owe any money to anyone else."

I was sad when visiting hours were over and we were forced to say good-bye to our friend.

"Maria, don't worry about anything," I assured her. "Everything will be fine."

She grasped my hands, as if she really did not want to let go. I explained to her that I was unable to visit her the next afternoon, but would return in the evening.

The following day there were many demands at the store that required my attention. At 5:30, I was in the rear of the store when I smelled a familiar odor: the distinctive scent of the Intensive Care Unit. Then the air grew cold. I called one of my employees, Irene, to come to where I stood and asked her what she smelled.

"Disinfectant ... like in a hospital," she replied.

"Maria came to say good-bye," I said.

I frantically called the hospital and asked about Maria's condition. The switchboard operator reported that she was resting comfortably.

I called back repeatedly within the next fifteen minutes and filled with dread, asked the same question. I received the same reply, but with each phone call the switchboard operator was becoming more and more irritated. I asked Irene to place a call and she, too, heard the same reply, "Resting comfortably."

Finally, I dialed the hospital one last time. I apologized for my persistence and explained that I was bringing an elderly friend with me to the hospital, and that she had a very bad heart.

"When I knock on the door, the nurse is going to tell me that Maria has passed away, and she will ask why I was not notified," I predicted. I hoped that by explaining my premonition that the operator would cooperate.

"I told you that she was resting comfortably," she snapped. "It's probably your imagination."

With that she disconnected the line and the phone went silent.

I picked up Bella, Maria's friend, without mentioning my premonition, and we drove to the hospital.

Arriving at the front door, we entered and hurried to the Intensive Care Unit. Just as I had predicted, the nurse met us at the door, and asked, "Weren't you telephoned?"

"No. Why?" I replied.

"Maria passed away at 5:30."

After I helped Bella recover from the shock of the sad news, I looked for the switchboard operator, ready to give her a piece of my mind.

"How did you know that Maria had passed away?" she asked. "I tried to call you, but you had already left. My condolences to you, but how did you know before I did?"

I looked at her without speaking, my eyes filled with tears, and I walked away.

After taking Bella home I returned to the store, called my wife and told her about Maria's death. Then I placed a call to the funeral director, Michael DeLuca, to make the funeral arrangements. He explained that I needed permission from Maria's will to make funeral arrangements since I was not a relative.

I walked the block to Maria's home. Although she had

given me the keys earlier, I felt uneasy entering her home knowing that she was no longer there. I rang the bell and her boarder came to the door.

I explained that Maria had passed away and I needed to get something from the kitchen. The kitchen felt empty without Maria's familiar presence and I picked up her red makeup case and placed it on the table. My heart pounding, I pushed the button to open the case, but it would not budge. I tried several times and still it would not open. I made a final attempt, and it seemed as if the lid flew open in my hands.

I emptied the contents including her tarot cards and religious paraphernalia. At the bottom I found her will, the deed to the cemetery plot, and the bill from her husband's funeral. I removed all the papers I needed, and with great care, replaced the rest of the contents.

Just as Maria predicted, eleven people attended her wake and she now rests next to her beloved Roberto.

In my grief, I let my heart take over and did not listen to my dear friend. I allowed her boarder to stay on for another month instead of asking him to leave immediately. I never found the black velvet bag containing the gold coins. All of Maria's furnishings, clothing and personal belongings were given to needy people. I believe in my heart that Maria would have wanted it that way.

I knew that somehow Maria was fully aware that all the wonderful things she had predicted for me would come true. I remembered the day we sat in her living room and she waved her hand and started to speak Italian.

"Maria, you know I don't understand Italian," I interrupted.

"Oh, sorry Caro," she replied. "Your wife is going to have another baby."

"I do not think so, Maria," I said. "Not now."

"And it's a girl," she pronounced.

This turned out to be one of Maria's most precious predictions. Our daughter, Michelle, was born within one year of Maria's words, on March 6, 1977.

A short time after Maria's passing, some of her clients came to my store and asked me if I would perform a reading for them. One woman I remember very clearly. I asked her why she came to me, since Maria was really the psychic.

"Maria told me a long time ago that you were a very gifted reader," she answered.

I believe that not only did Maria leave me her worldly belongings, but that she also opened the door to my understanding and openness to the universal messages I was receiving.

My only communication with Maria after her passing occurred in a dream. In it, Maria told me that she liked her house as it was and for me not to change it. A few days earlier I'd contemplated buying a larger headstone for Maria and her husband. After Maria's message via the dream, I decided to leave the original headstone.

Chapter 13

Having Insight

It would seem that having insight or the ability to see future events would ease life's hard lessons and would bring rewards. Unfortunately, this is not always true. In my experience, although I can see into the future, I cannot always detach myself emotionally to be objective enough to act on my perceptions.

In January of 1978, for the first time in my life, I felt suicidal. At the time I was coping with a serious stomach ailment. My doctor had ordered extensive testing and told me that there was a possibility that the tests would detect cancer. I dreaded putting my wife and children through a slow, agonizing illness and became more and more distraught.

One night before bed, I knelt down and prayed that the Angel of Death would visit me. I knew I could not commit suicide by my own hand, but actually when I prayed for the Angel of Death it was a form of "mental" suicide.

The same night I woke to feel a presence in the room. As I opened my eyes, there by the side of my bed stood a very tall figure. It put out its hand, and having no fear, I placed my hand in his.

"I come to answer your prayers," the voice murmured.

Next I felt myself lifted from the bed. It was at that moment as I floated above my sleeping wife that I realized I was not ready to die. Panicked, I struggled to free myself from my visitor's grip. However, the mysterious figure, still loomed before me.

"I am not ready to go," I said. "It is just that I don't want my family to watch me suffer."

The voice spoke, vibrating with love, "You have much work on earth to do. Clear your mind of any disease."

My movements rocked the bed, waking my wife. Startled, she yelled, "Why are you bouncing all over the place?"

"You're worried about me bouncing and they're coming to take me."

"Ed, you're just having a nightmare," she said. "Just go back to sleep."

A few weeks after this incident I received the results of my medical tests. Naturally, I was happy that the Angel of Death did not take me because the tests showed a small benign growth, but no real threat to my life.

This was a turning point for me and I became more sensitive to people's needs. I began giving readings using tarot cards and by interpreting the information in the palms of my clients. Instead of asking for a fee in return for the reading, I requested that they say a prayer as their payment. Sometimes I met people who were contemplating suicide, and from my experience, I worked closely with them. I never asked the person if he was considering suicide.

Instead, I would gently probe to determine whether he was struggling with thoughts about remaining on the earthplane. Then I would remind him of all the wonderful things in his life and all the people who loved him. I knew that he and others had the right to feel their pain, but I had to convince them to find a way to learn from their experiences.

For example, a young man came to see me. As he spoke, his calm words were quite different from the vibrations I was receiving. We discussed his father's passing and how difficult it was for him, because his finances changed after his father's death. It seemed that no matter how hard he tried, he became mired deeper and deeper in debt. I asked him if his financial problems were why he was struggling with whether or not to remain on the earthplane. His eyes brimmed with tears as he asked me what I meant. I knew he understood me so I asked him if he was suicidal. He broke down, weeping, and told me that suicide was his only way out of his problems. I asked him if he ever considered his mother's feelings and he admitted he hadn't. After he calmed down I instructed him to close his eyes and take in long, deep breaths.

Next I asked him to imagine his mother's face and how she would feel when she found his lifeless body. He sobbed harder. Once again, when he was calm I asked him to do the breathing exercise again and to summon a vision of himself two years in the future. I asked him to look ahead at his financial situation and he told me he saw himself no longer in debt. I asked him to breathe in his vision of no more money troubles and told him that he was capable of manifesting whatever he needed. I still occasionally see my client and he is extremely successful.

I do a lot of thinking as I commute from Staten Island to Brooklyn each day. One winter morning, as I drove toward my store I mulled over the dream I remembered from the previous night. I could not understand the meaning of the dream and it puzzled me. In it, I saw a young man, of about nineteen, with his arms raised. He held a gun in his right hand, and I heard his words, "This is my surprise and I want a bow on my casket."

I had awakened from the dream at 2:00 AM wondering why I was dreaming about John. I also wondered if I should call his parents and tell them about my dream? John's parents, Linda and Ed, owned a variety store across the street from my business.

Unfortunately, I never made the phone call. When I arrived at the store I discovered there was no need to decipher the dream. John had died from a gunshot wound. I was angry with myself because I thought that if I had called his parents when I awoke, maybe I could have somehow prevented their son's untimely death.

This was a very important lesson for me: that is was necessary to act on the warnings and symbols in my dreams.

There were times I thought that God was cruel to allow these tragedies. Children were born blind and crippled and I was often unable to help people cope with their pain. What I have since learned is that since God has given us free will, then we must think for ourselves and make our own karmic decisions.

It would be less than two months after John's death that I had another nocturnal visitor. Waking, I saw a shadow in the doorway of my bedroom. Someone had come to say good bye. However, as soon as I spotted the fleeting shadow, it disappeared. The next morning while driving to the store, I passed a catering business and realized that the owner was my late night visitor.

To everyone, the owner, Jim, was a tough guy. All

Jim's employees jumped to attention when he entered a room. Yet, you might say that Jim saved my life.

I was alone in my store when a man entered with his hand in his pocket acting as if he held a gun. He told me he was going to rob me, and demanded that I give him whatever cash I had on hand. As the robber finished his threat, Jim happened to walk into the store. He seemed to instantly understand what was taking place, and threatened the would-be thief, warning him that he was going to split his head open and ordered him to leave. I never saw anybody run so fast. Jim laughed as if he had just won a long shot.

That morning, the same day that Jim appeared earlier in my store to banish the thief, I learned that my instincts were correct. Jim had already passed away when he appeared the next day to rout the thug. His death had occurred the night before, probably not long before he visited me in my bedroom to say good-bye.

A few weeks after Jim's funeral I had another visit from him and he asked me to help his family. He told me there was a lot of confusion since his death, and his family was not adjusting well. I called Jim's daughter, Stephanie, and told her about her father's message. She asked me if I could come to her home.

When I arrived I rang the doorbell. There was no answer. I went back to my car to wait for her. As I looked back towards the house, I was shocked to witness a fire starting inside the house. I ran from my car, hurried to the house and peered through the window. There was no fire. Just then Stephanie arrived and I told her what I had seen. "Boy, don't you have an imagination," she laughed.

She wanted to know if I felt her father's presence in her home. When I told her that I sensed her father near by she spoke again.

"Not only do I feel my father's presence," Stephanie said. "But I smell his cologne."

The reason Stephanie had called me, I discovered, was to ask for my assistance to locate an article belonging to her father. I gave her detailed information about the missing article and later discovered the information I gave her was correct.

We discussed her mother's distress and I warned Stephanie that she needed to watch her mother closely.

Then the next day, Stephanie called me to tell me that a fire started in her kitchen shortly after I left her.

It was only a month after speaking with Stephanie that she called to tell me that her mother wanted to commit suicide, and begged me to please help her. For the next two years, I worked in person and spent a lot of time on the telephone guiding Stephanie's mother through her pain.

Often my family visited me at my store. On one occasion, on a busy Saturday, the day before Easter 1980, my Uncle John and Aunt May were visiting with my grandparents for the holiday. Since they were not staying over for Easter Sunday, they dropped by the store to say hello to my mother.

In an Italian family there are always lots of hugs and kisses when we greet each other. When I hugged my Uncle John, I placed my hands on his back and sensed through my hands a massive, white, jello-like substance under his skin. I did not mention my discovery to my aunt and uncle. But, I believed that I needed to share my concerns with my mother. After mulling it over for several hours I finally told Mom that I needed to speak with her.

"Mom," I began. "I don't want to say anything that's going to hurt you. But Uncle John has lung cancer."

Her eyes immediately welled up with tears.

"Why? Did Aunt May tell you that?" she asked. "Or did my brother?"

"No, Mom, I could feel it in my hands."

By this time my mother knew better than to shrug off my intuition. I warned her only because I thought it best she knew.

"Ed, what do you think the outcome will be?" she asked.

"Uncle John is going to have lung surgery," I assured her. "He's certainly not ready to die."

Not long after Easter, Uncle John had a lung removed, then began chemotherapy. When the family learned that Uncle John needed the surgery, my mother was prepared, although she was concerned. The surgery went well.

By May 1 of 1985, Uncle John's health was slipping. On that day, he made a strange statement, which none of his family understood: "Thirteen pink stones."

On the morning of May 13, I received a phone call telling me that he was failing. I went to pick up my cousin, Linda, and we drove together to the hospital in New Jersey. As we were about fifteen minutes into the drive I told Linda that I hoped I was wrong, but Uncle John had just passed away.

When we arrived at the hospital we were ushered to a waiting room, then the head nurse told us that Uncle John had died an hour earlier.

His funeral was very sad. Watching my grandparents say good-bye to their son was hard for all of us. As we arrived at his graveside, I noticed the mausoleum was made of pink marble. I then realized what my uncle had meant thirteen days earlier when he said, "Thirteen pink stones." He was pronouncing his own death date, the thirteenth, and describing the opening to his crypt which was made of pink marble.

After Uncle John's funeral service, family and friends gathered at my aunt's home. By this time it was common knowledge among my cousins and some of my older family members that I was able to see into the future, as well as the past.

My cousin Charlie must have mentioned this to his friend, Buddy, because Buddy asked me if I would mind telling him something about his future.

I asked Buddy for permission to place my fingers in the center of his palm. I went on to explain that this touch connected me with his vibration. I believe that this is kind of a conduit, like putting an electrical plug into an outlet so that the current goes in a full cycle.

Buddy held out his hand and I began the reading.

As I was given information, I asked him if he preferred that the reading be held in private. He assured me that he had nothing to hide. I was uneasy about giving him information since I did not want to cause him any pain. I asked again if he was certain he wanted to hear what I had to say and he replied affirmatively.

I started to describe a letter he had recently received. I described how when he opened the letter he could not stop crying.

Buddy looked at me in amazement. "What does the letter say?" he asked.

"It is about your disease," I answered.

"Ed, you are absolutely correct." He asked, "Will my life be short?"

I felt no need to tell him when his life would be over. Instead I replied, "Life is never short, it's only when we look ahead and don't enjoy the moments of today. Trust in God."

I didn't spend time with Buddy after our meeting until two days before he passed away, when again I had a premonition. I called my Aunt Carol. "Charlie's friend, Buddy, will pass away soon. Your son needs you."

Later that day my aunt arrived at Charles' home; Buddy passed away two days later.

Those of us who are sensitive to spirits of the dead often attract those who have a difficult time making the transition from life as we know it to the unknown. Often, people who have died, but are distraught because they think they have left unfinished business on earth, attempt to delay or resist their passage to the beyond. The story that follows relates how one such reluctant spirit desperately sought to reverse the circumstances of his death.

An Early Morning Phone Call

I learned about the death of Carl from his widow in Seattle several years after the event. She related the story of an astonishing telephone call from a friend three thousand miles away barely twelve hours after her husband's demise.

Margaret, still stunned and bewildered by the violent death of her husband the previous morning, had fallen into an exhausted sleep after a confusing, depressing day of trying to find answers to questions about the reason for her husband's death. They were questions that baffled and disturbed her and plunged her deeper into grief and misery.

When the telephone on her bedstand rang at two o'clock in the morning, she groped for the receiver, groggy and disoriented. Still drugged with sleep, unaware of the early morning hour, she thought the telephone ringing was another condolence call. During the day there had been dozens of expressions of shock and sympathy from friends and relatives.

When she sat up in bed to place the receiver against her ear, she noticed the early hour on her bedside clock.

Margaret was surprised and mystified when her caller turned out to be a family friend, Natalie, but what was she doing on the phone from New York at such an ungodly hour?

She had barely acknowledged Natalie's greeting when her friend, with unaccustomed rude urgency, said, "Margaret, I have to talk with Carl. I know it's early, but I've got to talk with him! Please put him on the phone."

Natalie, a woman who had stayed with Margaret and Carl for a prolonged period two years previously, had proven to be a provocative house guest with strong spiritual leanings and remarkable powers of clairvoyance that were first demonstrated to Margaret one day when the two were lingering over breakfast coffee.

Natalie had suddenly put her cup down firmly on the breakfast table and, with a strange light in her eyes, had turned to Margaret and said, "Irene is dead."

"What do you mean? You're crazy! How would you know such a thing? I just talked to her yesterday!"

Natalie was referring to a dear friend of Margaret's who had introduced Natalie to Margaret originally. She had moved to Los Angeles from Seattle to assist her daughter in a medical subscription business. Margaret and Irene had been close friends since they studied together years before at the University of Washington.

Unmoved by Margaret's dismayed rejection of her announcement, Natalie had said softly, "I'm sorry you took the news badly, but it's true. Irene's dead. I can't tell you how I know, but she's gone."

Still unbelieving, but worried and concerned, Margaret had called Irene's number in Los Angeles. When the phone was answered, she immediately recognized Sally, Irene's daughter.

"Sally, is your mother all right? It's Margaret."

"Oh, Margaret," Sally cried, "I'm so glad it's you. Mom died this morning. A stroke. I don't know what to do! Will you come?"

Now, two years later, with Natalie's former prediction of Irene's death in her mind as a warning, Margaret said to her friend on the Atlantic coast, "Why such a hurry to speak to Carl? Why are you so disturbed?"

There was a long moment of hesitation on the line before Natalie's voice came back. "Margaret, I was awakened just a few minutes ago. At first, I thought it was a dream, then I realized it wasn't. It was Carl. He was standing at the foot of my bed. His head was thickly bandaged and blood had soaked through the gauze and was running down his face.

"At first, I thought it couldn't be Carl because he was wearing a shadow plaid suit with a paisley tie. And he never dressed like that. He always wore conservative suits, pin-striped blue or gray. Then, I realized it was him.

"Oh, Margaret, his eyes were terrible to look at, full of pain and regret when he asked for help. He was desperate and kept saying, 'Help me, Natalie. Help me get back. I've done something awful and I have to get back. I've made a terrible mistake.'

"He disappeared and then came back again, in a few minutes. He kept pleading for me to help him. He was so pitiful and desperate, I thought my heart would break. I couldn't make up my mind whether I was dreaming, or his visit was real. I knew I had to call and find out what was tormenting him. Is he there?"

Margaret sighed deeply from the hard knot of sadness and hurt that burned in her chest and threatened to engulf her with grief so profound that she thought she would drown from the flood of unshed tears. She took a deep, ragged breath, then said shakily to Natalie, "Oh, my dear, he's not here anymore. He went to his office early yesterday morning, sat at his desk, put a gun to his head and pulled the trigger. He's dead, Natalie. And Natalie, just yesterday morning he dressed in a new shadow plaid suit he had bought, and put on a silly paisley tie. He looked so different, as if he wasn't himself at all. Of course, he wasn't. You had no way of knowing what happened. It hasn't been on the news, or anything like that."

It was several days after Natalie's call that Margaret thought about her husband's visitation to their friend in New York. Not for a moment did she doubt his appearance in Natalie's bedroom, begging her for help to return from across the gulf of the dead.

Margaret concluded that Carl's desperate appearance after he'd killed himself was his renunciation of his act and a prayer for forgiveness. He had gone to the one person he knew of who would not have dismissed his nocturnal vision as an aberration or bad dream that should be ignored.

As she sat alone in her bedroom after Carl's funeral, after all the busy-ness and ceremony and etiquette of death observance had been dutifully completed, and after she had overcome her own exhaustion in a deep, healing sleep, Margaret made a tentative peace with her husband's suicide. She accepted that he had killed himself because of cruel changes in the executive lineup at the corporation to which he had devoted twenty-five years of his life. He was being mercilessly pushed out, discarded, and he was terrified of the future.

She had accepted this explanation with irony, deep regret for him and a certain bitterness over his wasting his life because he felt desperately inadequate compared to men who were far less than him, and could think of no solution but to arrange for his own absence.

More significant and deeply profound to her was the fact of his strange appearance in the New York apartment of their friend after he had died. She had always believed a little that life continued after death, but now her absent husband had left her with a gift he had not intended — the promise — by his post-demise materialization, of a certainty that life was ongoing. Death was but a stage in human development. It was a sweet knowledge for Margaret and it gave her husband's departed life a greater meaning than the rude ending in his office.

Chapter 14

Faith

By April of 1984 I was having strong visions once again that I would lose someone who I loved very dearly. The visions were of my mother and they were letting me know that she would be leaving on April 3, 1987. I didn't tell her about my visions. Concerned, I kept asking her if she would go to the doctor for a checkup, but she insisted that there was nothing wrong with her. For the next two months, as the thought of losing her became stronger, I tried to push what I knew was going to happen from my mind and say a prayer.

Two months later, in June, my mother had to be rushed to Lutheran Medical Center. After extensive testing, her doctor informed us that she had a tumor lodged in the bronchial tube in her lung and the only way they could stop its growth was with radiation treatment. If she did not receive immediate treatment, she would only have three days to live.

As her treatment began we learned how strong she really was, and her strength gave us the courage to hold on to our faith.

As the hours of the next three days crawled past, I felt like a prisoner awaiting the electric chair. Every moment felt like hours. I was grateful when the three days were over and my mother was still alive, but the following days were just as draining.

Finally, we received word from the doctor that he wanted to speak with us. He reassured us that the tumor had started to shrink. We were truly elated by this news.

Unfortunately, there was a catch — the kind of cancer that plagued my mother would have to be monitored very carefully. It could come back. If there were signs of the slightest bit of pain in any part of her body, she would have to be examined immediately. According to the doctor, her type of cancer showed no mercy, engulfing the entire body like a piranha attacking.

As her treatments progressed, I noticed changes in my mother: her sweet-sounding voice took on a gravelly tone. Yet through it all she never complained. In fact, she steadfastly assured me that she would be fine.

We were overjoyed when she was released from the hospital five weeks later. My sister, Connie, prepared her home for my mother and made arrangements to transport her to the hospital for continued radiation treatments. As the weeks went by her treatments became a normal part of our lives.

By the New Year of 1985, Mom seemed to be back to normal and the treatments were long over. The only reminder of her ordeal was the change in her voice. God was truly on my mother's side as her health remained stable until October of 1986, when she began her second battle with cancer.

We knew after the first radiation treatments that she was not a candidate for more radiology. We were told that her lungs were like tissue paper and half of one lung needed to be removed. The surgery was scheduled for 9:00 AM.

The day of the surgery, Connie and I went to the hospital. When we arrived the nurse told us our mother had already been wheeled into surgery.

Trying to remain calm during a crisis is not one of my best traits. As we waited for Dr. Connelly to report the outcome of my mother's lung surgery, my brother, Anthony, talked to me, but so intense was my concentration on my mom's outcome that his words passed over my head. My eyes were glued to the shiny elevator doors, where I expected to see the doctor appear. The doors seemed to draw me like a magnet for I was unable to focus on anything else. Each time they slid open, my mind raced with anticipation.

My life had been filled with visions and premonitions, both wonderful and sad. Yet, on this day as my mother lay ill, I did not want to know if God had made his final decision to reach out and call her home.

It was in this frame of mind, with my eyes closed, that I heard a familiar voice from the past, a voice from childhood which I thought I had long forgotten.

"It is not her time," the voice whispered. "Look within yourself, and you will know the answer."

When my mother's operation was over, Dr. Connelly came to tell us that he believed the surgery was successful. Yet as I looked at the doctor, in my heart I knew he was not telling us the whole truth.

On my way home I thought of how much paper work waited for me at the store before I could return to the hospital during visiting hours to see Mom when she was awake and recovering. There was bookkeeping to be done and checks needed to be written, so I quickly planned my day in my head.

I left the house early the next morning to accomplish all the chores at the store. I sat down with the checkbook to pay bills and on the first check I wrote I discovered I had post-dated the check by about six months. I had written April 3, 1987. Was this another way for the Universe to give me confirmation of my previous vision, that my mother would leave us on that date?

I finished my tasks at the store and left for Sloan Kettering Hospital. Mom looked drained and exhausted when I saw her. It was apparent that she was still in a lot of pain. I kissed her hello and she told me that her doctor had informed her that the surgery went well.

"Now, I want to know what you think," she said.

"Mom, Dr. Connelly said everything went well, that's exactly what he told us."

"I am not talking about what the doctor had to say," she insisted. "I want to know what *you* have to say."

"Mom, I have nothing different to say than what the doctor told you."

"Are you sure?"

"Mom, you'll be out of the hospital soon enough."

"I need to be home to take care of Prudence."

"Mom, you'll be taking care of Prudence for as long as necessary."

The expression on my mother's face told me that she knew I was not telling the truth.

When she was finally released from the hospital, she returned quickly to her normal affairs, making plans with her granddaughter Prudence, our daughter named after my wife, and venturing on outings with her friends. Mom cherished her independence, preferring to drive herself places and not rely on others to chauffeur her. She was also spending one day a week in the store answering the telephone.

As promised, Mom traveled to Florida with little Prudence at the end of the school year. Before the trip she had a checkup at Sloan Kettering and was given a clean bill of health and told there wasn't a trace of cancer in her lungs. An appointment was made for a subsequent examination in early December.

As Christmas grew closer, Mom was busy doing her Christmas shopping and decorating her house. Christmas was her favorite time of year.

As Mom and Connie sat in Dr. Richard's office conferring over details, he suggested that she be admitted to Sloan Kettering for the new tests. Mom refused, informing him that Christmas was only two weeks away and she wanted to spend it with her family. However, she promised to enter the hospital for tests right after the New Year.

When Christmas Eve came my home was completely decorated for the festive holiday. The ten-foot tree was a dazzling array of decorations and lights, garlands graced the stairway, poinsettia stood by the fireplace, and all the Christmas stockings hung on the mantle.

As I think back to that Christmas Eve, I realize that my mother needed to express her emotions as all of us gathered. Yet Mom must have realized that we were all fighting with our fears, emotions, and tears as well. Mom announced proudly that the gift she brought was for both Prudence, and myself. My wife understood that I should open this final Christmas gift from my mother. With my wife's kind insistence, I unwrapped and opened the package. I reached in and carefully took out tissue-wrapped bundles. The first figure was the Blessed Mother, and then I unwrapped a complete nativity scene. As I held the small figurine of Mary in my hand, I turned it over. It was inscribed, "Christmas 1986, Mom." As hard as we tried, none of us could hold back the tears.

As I knelt down to hug my mother, I told her how much I loved her and how much I would cherish her thoughtful gift, hand-crafted with tenderness and love. "Mom, we're only crying out of joy," I assured her. "You're going to be perfectly fine."

Once again she looked directly in my eyes and said, "Only you know if that's true."

I could see that she was searching my face for the truth. Looking back, I realize that it was wise at the beginning of the evening to allow our emotions to flow. With them released, it was easier to laugh and enjoy our holiday together. During the festive Christmas dinner later we served everything that Mom enjoyed: lobster oreganato, crabs in red sauce, shrimp scampi, mussels in light red sauce and her favorite, *fruitta de mar,* which translates to fruit of the sea, an assorted fish salad.

A week later, we all watched Dick Clark's New Year's celebration until the ball dropped at Times Square, and we heard church bells ring. There were tears for husbands, fathers and brothers who had walked into God's light. My own tears wet my eyes, for I knew that the end of my mother's time on earth was "just a breath away." We all hugged and kissed and expressed our love for one another.

Later, after midnight as my mother drove away, I watched the car make a left turn at the corner and I knew that it would be the last time that she would spend the holidays with us.

Thursday, when she was scheduled to begin her tests, came too quickly, but I arrived at my mother's home at nine in the morning to drive her to the hospital. When we arrived and Mom walked through the doors, I could actually see her energy shift. I knew then that she would never leave the hospital walking on her own two feet.

On January 17 when I visited her, she wished me "happy birthday" and handed me a card and a small box wrapped in gold foil paper.

"I wanted to give you something special for your fortieth birthday," she said.

Again, I tried to hide my emotions. I truly wanted to believe what the doctor had told me earlier that day, that Mom was going to be fine. He had explained that she was going to be fitted with a back brace which would relieve the pressure on her sciatic nerve. He also said that she would be released from the hospital as soon as the brace arrived.

"Mom, I received a wonderful birthday present when I spoke to the doctor today. After you get the back brace, you are going home."

She just looked at me, nodding in seeming agreement, but there was no smile. She insisted I open the box.

The box contained a disk made of black onyx imprinted with the face of Christ.

"I wanted you to have something very special for this birthday," she explained.

When visiting hours were over Mom insisted that I leave, but I protested.

"I always stay until the guard comes and says I have to leave."

"Well, tonight I'm a little tired," she answered. "I want to get some sleep. So you leave now and I'll see you tomorrow."

Reluctantly, I left, convinced in my heart that my mother had conspired with her doctor for him to tell me that everything was fine in order to make my fortieth birthday free of worries.

For Valentine's Day we sent Mom a dozen roses along with a three foot, heart-shaped Mylar balloon which was tied to the end of her hospital bed. It was in mid-February that our conversations took a sudden change. She called me at work one day and said she needed to see me. When I arrived at the hospital, I knew from my mother's questions that she had wholly accepted the unusual gift that God had given me.

"I need to ask you something," she began. "But I don't want you to become upset."

"Mom, what do you have to ask me?"

"Tell me how to die," she said. "I've never done this before."

Stunned, I could feel a shocked expression come over my face.

"Tell me how to die," she repeated. "I've never done this before."

At first I didn't know how to answer.

"How am I supposed to know?" I demanded. "I've never died before either."

"Oh, yes you have," she assured me. "In many past lifetimes."

After I heard the words, "in many lifetimes," I began to describe to her what she should expect. I explained that when it was her time to leave she should simply walk toward the light and keep on walking. I told her that there would be others on the other side to greet her and that she would recognize each person who came to help her. I assured her that she would recognize her "helpers" by the essence they radiated, which was pure love. We discussed the possibility that she would hear the harps of the angels guiding each step she took into the doorway of light that opens to the heavenly realm. This light, I said, was emitted from the souls who have passed over before, a kind of shower of love.

I explained to my mother that while she was on her journey she would feel the presence of those she left behind but should not allow our love to hold her earthbound. I assured her that she would let us know when her transition was complete.

From that day, as time passed, our conversations became centered on spiritual issues. Everything that I believed and had witnessed all of my life, my mother was now confirming. Her experiences as she neared death gave me answers to the great mystery of life and death. At times my mind could not believe what my ears were hearing. If there were not so much pain involved, I would have been very grateful for my mother's wisdom. It was only later that I realized that my mother had become my greatest teacher.

One day while visiting her, she asked me to draw the drape that hung between her bed and the bed of woman next to her.

"Mom, why are we closing the drape?" I asked.

When the drapes were closed to her satisfaction she whispered, "I don't want to mix her company with mine."

I was certain that the woman in the next bed was alone. Yet to be certain I peeked outside of the drape. "Mom, the lady is by herself, there's no one there."

However, Mom insisted that there was someone with her roommate.

"Okay, if there is somebody there," I challenged. "What does he look like?"

She described a man, about five feet tall, with a pencil-thin mustache. She also added that her roommate had a blood disorder and that the man was waiting patiently for her to accompany him. At times, my psychic knowing was overwhelmed by emotion, but I just let my mother go on with her story and hoped that her reasserted cancer had not spread to her brain. Later, when the children of the woman in the next bed arrived to visit, I waited for the opportunity to speak to her son alone. As soon as he left the room, I followed and struggled with how to broach the subject.

"I believe my mother recognizes your mother from the neighborhood," I said.

Then I described the gentleman who my mother claimed she had seen in the room.

"That was my father," the son replied. "He died twenty years ago."

I simply stared at him, yet I still needed to confirm my mother's information about his mother's illness.

"Will your mother be going home soon?" I asked.

He answered, "I hope so, but my mother has leukemia."

Within three days the woman passed over; the cause of her death: leukemia.

Chapter 15

My Mother,
My Teacher

In early March, Mom's lungs were x-rayed. When I arrived at the hospital to visit she told me that the x-ray film clearly showed deterioration in her right lung and spread of the cancer into her left lung. Then she said that, although she could live for a long time, her choice was to die.

"Mom, who told you this?" I asked.

She just looked at me without answering. I asked again, but she did not answer. I excused myself, telling her that I was going to the cafeteria, but I really intended to speak to her doctor.

In his office when we met, I saw kindness in his face, but I was angry that he would share the x-ray results with my mother before consulting her family. Previously, I had been emphatic that she was not to know how serious her illness was. He patiently listened as I berated him for informing my mother without our permission.

Gently he said, "I'm sorry, but I haven't told your mother anything. The results of the x-rays aren't in yet. They won't be here for a few more hours."

I asked if he was sure and if it was possible that someone else could have told her about what the x-ray showed.

He assured me that the results would be delivered directly to him, then he would discuss them with Dr. Tricarico and finally with me.

Baffled, I repeated what my mother had told me and I asked again if he was certain that no one had revealed any information to her.

He shook his head and said, "Absolutely not."

I was still beside myself over Mom's news and questioned her when I returned to her room. I asked how she'd obtained the information. She assured me that the results didn't come from her doctor.

"If he didn't tell you, then who did?"

She hesitated for a moment, then looked directly into my eyes. You would think after all my psychic experience I would have been prepared for her answer; "Your father and my brother John."

"How did Daddy get in the room?" I questioned. "Through the door?"

With a child-like gesture, she pointed toward the ceiling. "There, there is the door," she explained.

"Mom, what door?" I asked bewildered.

"There is a door, and your father and Uncle John came through. I have been telling you to move that big balloon because it blocks the view," she said.

"Mom," I went on, "is that why you are always looking up at the ceiling?"

"Yes," she replied. "Now will you remove the

balloon? It's not that I don't love the present, but I have to look into the doorway."

Several hours later I was called into the hallway by both her doctors. They confirmed the x-ray results my mother had already described.

"I do not know how your mother got the results before I did," her doctor said, clearly baffled.

Once again, my mother, my teacher, confirmed for me that other dimensions are a reality.

When no one was around, Mom would ask me to tell her the story of the light after death, which I had described to her earlier. She wanted to make certain that she would not forget anything, so I repeated what I had told her. One day, she said to me, "When my time is near, I wish for no one to be in the room. If any of you are present, my love for you will stop me from going."

As the month of March drew to a close, I knew in my heart that Mother's time was closer. However, her doctors insisted that she would live for quite some time and were deciding whether to move her to the terminally-ill ward and suggested that later we should place her in a hospice.

During this period I was part owner of a bridal salon. In the last week of March my partner, Mike, brought in a yard of pale blue French silk embossed with tear drops of deep blue and silver. I asked him to order ten yards of the fabric for me.

I met with Lilian, a seamstress, and we designed my mother's farewell dress. Lilian asked me if I wanted to see the dress when it was completed. I said that the only time I wanted to see the dress was when my mother was wearing it.

"How much time do I have to make this dress?"

"Not very much time at all."

When I arrived at the hospital that day, I spotted my brother and sister, Anthony and Connie, in the cafeteria and told them about the dress. Surprisingly, they took my news well. "Do you think Mom's time is soon?" Anthony asked.

I nodded yes. I explained that she had made plans for all the details of her funeral attire including her hair, makeup and nail polish, right down to her undergarments. My mother was determined to leave the earth with dignity. She had even chosen a funeral home.

While it was difficult to hear my mother plan these intimate arrangements, I was grateful and relieved that she had made her own decisions.

As I repeated our conversation, Anthony and Connie both seemed surprised that she would have such a conversation with me. At the time none of us realized that she was guiding me toward the work that I do today. I had always doubted whether I was truly capable of communicating with those who had passed over, despite happenings which demonstrated the reappearance of those who had died. Now, I was witnessing my mother's conversations with the other side and ultimately this fact encouraged me to work with my gift.

After our talk, we went upstairs to visit our mother and she took her usual single sip from her favorite strawberry malted. Mom asked Anthony and Connie to leave her alone with me for a minute, so that we could speak privately.

"When will my dress be complete?" she asked.

"Mom, what dress?"

"The dress you're having made for me; the blue one."

"Mom, I don't know what you're talking about."

While I felt uneasy about lying to Mom, I still couldn't summon the courage to tell her about the dress.

"When it's finished I want to see it," she instructed. "And if you can't bring me the dress, bring me a piece of the fabric."

"Mom, there is no dress," I insisted.

"Yes there is. You just finished telling your brother and sister about it."

"How do you know what we discussed? We were five floors below you."

Once again, she pointed upward to that invisible doorway and said, "Your father."

When I left her that evening she reminded me again to bring her a piece of the silk fabric.

On the fourth floor of the hospital Mrs. La Gravanece, who was the mother of one of my employees, lay ill. She had been hospitalized for about two weeks, then passed away during the night. When I reached the hospital on the following afternoon the first thing my mother told me was that a friend of hers had passed away.

"Who called you and told you the news?" I asked.

"No one called me," she answered.

I was a bit confused. The only person I knew who had recently passed away was Irene's mother, Mrs. La Gravanece. Irene worked for me.

"Irene won't be stopping to see me anymore. Her mother passed away."

"Mom, how do you know?"

"She came to say good-bye," she said.

"Who came to say good-bye?" I asked.

"Irene's mother. She told me she wasn't sorry she had to go, to let Irene know that she was fine."

When I went to Mrs. La Gravanece's wake, I relayed my mother's message to Irene. Through her tears she expressed her gratitude at my words since she was upset that when her mother passed over she was alone.

Later that evening, I phoned the private nurse, Avis, who attended my mother, to see how she was doing and Avis informed me that my mother wanted to speak with me.

During the conversation with my mother she made a curious request; she asked me to bring three white buttons, a needle and white thread to the hospital the following day. When I asked why she needed these things, she explained that she had promised the lady she would sew on her three white buttons.

I did not question her any further and promised to bring the buttons. When I arrived at the hospital the next day she immediately asked me for the buttons, needle and thread.

"The lady said she will return soon, so I want to have them here when she comes back," Mom told me.

I asked her, "Who is the lady?

"The lady said she'll come back to help me."

"When is she coming back?" I asked, still puzzled.

"When it's my time she told me she would return," Mom replied.

Death bed visions sometimes come from angelic figures sent by a loved one who has passed over earlier, or the presence can be in the form of a religious figure such as Jesus, Moses or the Blessed Mother. I later realized my mother was referring to the Blessed Mother and that the three buttons she requested signified the third day of April.

As the final weekend of March neared, Mom asked to speak to each one of her family individually, and announced to each of us that she was going to die. My mother spoke to my sister first. I do not know the details of her conversation, only that she told Connie that she would take over the role of mother to the family and watch over all of us.

One by one we were given our final instructions.

When it was my turn, she said, "I really have nothing to say to you. I love you and I wish things could have been different. It's not that I love the others less, but I'll always love you more. When the time comes, I don't want you to spend too much money."

"Mom, I just want you to remember that when it's my time, I want you to be there in the light to help guide me through."

After our exchange, the rest of my family came back into the room. One of the nurses was summoned because Mom's vital signs were dropping. With growing dread I knew I was not ready yet to hand her over to God. Desperately trying to win time, I told her that she needed to speak to her sister, Rosalie. I dialed my aunt's number and they spoke, then we placed a call to her brother, Joe. Her final phone call was to my sister, Carol. Carol begged her to hang on a few more days until she flew in from Florida.

For the next few days Mom continued to speak openly about her passing and inquire if her dress was finished.

"When it's time for me to go, I have to do this by myself," she reminded me. "I don't wish to have anyone there."

When Carol finally arrived from Florida it seemed that my mother had made a full recovery. She even asked Carol to put on her eye shadow and lipstick. When I walked into the room I was stunned, I had not seen my mother look so well in months. With her makeup on, there were no telltale signs of her illness. Even her manner had changed and she was more alert, talkative, and never mentioned dying. Carol turned to me and said, "Doesn't Mommy look beautiful?"

It was not that I did not want my mother to look beautiful and healthy, I had grown accustomed to seeing her in pain. Now to see her look well and yet know that she was dying, made me briefly believe that she was not really sick. But then Carol removed the makeup and it was as if the clock had struck twelve. Just like the Cinderella story, once again Mom looked like her former self, drained and weak.

When someone dies slowly, it is probably easier on the loved ones left behind than the sudden death without warning that shocks the survivors. Our family had months to grow accustomed to Mom's passing and to discuss all the wonderful things that she would witness and see in her next life. My mother's final wish was to die at home. I was determined to see that her wish was honored.

After I obtained her doctor's permission, my mother was released on April 2, 1987.

We arranged to have oxygen delivered, along with all the necessary prescriptions and equipment that was needed to keep her comfortable. As for me, I was not on hand to see her leave the hospital in a wheelchair. I simply could not cope with witnessing her weakness and frailty.

When the ambulance arrived in front of my mother's home, I was standing outside waiting for her. As a crowd gathered on the sidewalk, and the ambulance driver opened the door, I stepped in, and in keeping with her wishes, I asked the nurse to cover her completely with a blanket around her head to shield her from the crowd of people watching.

As we entered the hall to carry her up the stairs, I knew I would see my Great-Grandma Lily standing there. I could feel the terrible countdown starting. It would only be one more day before my mother passed over.

In a flash she was whisked upstairs and tucked into her bed. When she saw her emaciated reflection in the mirror, she wailed, "Oh my God, I didn't think it would be like this."

I did not mention to anyone that I'd spotted Great-Grandma Lily in the hall. After being home only about ten minutes, Mom asked to see her father. I went up to the next floor and brought Grandpa down to visit his failing daughter.

Mom asked me to watch over my grandparents and to make certain that they had everything they needed. We tried to make small talk with the family, but it was very difficult for everyone. When it was time for me to leave my mother reminded me that one day I would lie next to her and not to forget all that she had asked.

"And remember that I will love you for all eternity."

Although we were relieved that my mother was safely at home, for me the clock was moving too quickly. The next day was April 3. Before leaving the store the next morning, I instructed one of my employees to call the priest so that he could give my mother her last rites. When he arrived in Mom's room and began intoning the ancient ritual, his voice was very loud. When he called out my mother's name, she opened her eyes, looked toward him and waved him away. I am sure that he did not realize that she was preoccupied with aligning her inner vision to God's White Light. The priest finished the ritual, said his farewells and left.

Anthony and Connie were called; my other sister, Carol, had said her good-bye the previous afternoon, but was on her way back to New York after being notified of Mother's last hours.

As I greeted Connie at the door, I warned her that Mom was fading quickly. She nodded that she understood, bent and kissed my mother. She told her how much she loved her, then whispered that it was okay for her to go. There was no reply. Mom looked as if she were in a deep sleep.

As Connie straightened after her good-bye kiss, her starched collar caught my mother's eyelid. I saw that no longer was there a murky discoloration in Mom's eyes. They had returned to the clear blue I always remembered. This was my confirmation that my mother's transition was complete.

I took my turn with a farewell kiss and whispered all the things I wanted to say and reminded Mom that when it was my turn she had promised to be there to help me walk into the Light of God.

A moment later, I heard the phone ring and answered it. It was my sister Carol calling from Kennedy International Airport. "Mommy just passed away, didn't she?" Carol asked. "I saw her. She came to say good-bye to me at the airport."

I could hear her crying and asked her to come home as quickly as possible.

I stepped into the hallway as Anthony was running up the stairs yelling, "Did I make it, did I make it?"

When I answered that he was too late, we melted into each others arms and wept. When we entered the bedroom everyone started crying all over again. With each new arrival, the tears flowed again.

By Monday morning, all of us were exhausted, drained of emotion, and silently relieved that the wake was over and the burial would take place. None of us could tolerate the strain of another hour.

The last memory I have of the day we buried Mom was the stillness of the air and the sun glistening on the bed of pink roses placed on top of her casket.

After my mother passed on I had one curious dream about her. She was dressed all in white and was working in a veterinarian's office.

"Mom, what are you doing here?" I asked.

"All good things come in time."

"You haven't answered my question, Mom. What are you doing in a veterinarian's office?"

"All good things come in time," she replied again.

For the next couple of days the dream haunted me; what did it mean? I got my answer one morning when our beloved Shetland sheepdog Sandy died. I had to think about the connection between the dog and my dream, but finally understood that my mother's appearance in the vet's office was symbolic of the expression "All God's creatures go to heaven." Sandy had ascended.

One example of how spirits of the departed remind us to remember them happened in the person of a two-year-old.

My family still owns the building in which my grandparents and mother lived. The tenants who live on the top floor have a two-year-old child named Amanda.

During Mother's Day week, 1997, Amanda's parents believed that she was having an imaginary conversation. They heard Amanda say, "Mama, Mama, Mama."

Thinking Amanda was addressing her, Amanda's mother answered, "Yes Amanda."

Again Amanda said insistently, "No, Mama, Mama, Mama."

On Mother's Day the mystery was solved when the two-year-old came to my store to visit her father Billy, one of my employees. On the wall there was a photograph of my mother. Amanda looked up at the photograph, pointed and exclaimed, "Mama."

Then she looked around at smiled at the people in the store, pointed tenderly and repeated, "Mama, Mama, Mama."

The message the little one was bringing was unravelled: She had visited with my deceased mother and confirmed it by pointing to her photo in the store.

Chapter 16

The Fire

After the long drawn-out months of my mother's illness with no time for myself, I now had more hours available in the day than I was accustomed to. I found I did not know what to do with my time. And I discovered that there was little comfort from the pain of my loss.

As usual, there were customers to deal with, some who didn't know of my mother's passing. It was painful to have to answer their questions and to repeat the same story again and again. I learned that my mother touched many lives through her kindness, compassion and generosity.

During the next year, for reasons I didn't quite understand, it seemed that the Universe shut down my psychic awareness until a day in July of 1988. Evidently I needed to deal with the grief process; the various stages of anger and acceptance before my foresight would return.

After Mom's death, Connie moved into a new home and furnished it with things my mother had left behind for her. When I entered her house for the first time, I was apprehensive about seeing my mother's furniture in another setting. I walked into the kitchen and in my mind's eye I suddenly saw flames. I quickly pushed this disturbing image from my mind and said a prayer.

The next day I received a phone call at the store. A fire had engulfed a portion of Connie's home. I rushed over and was relieved that she was unhurt.

As I entered the house I wondered why I hadn't warned her the day before. The whole interior of the house was destroyed. The kitchen, where the fire began, was an ashen shell. The dining room was destroyed, except for the laminated prayer cards from my mother's funeral. They were untouched by the flames. Immediately, I remembered what my father told me on his last visit twenty-three years earlier: "One day all your mother's worldly possessions will burn."

As I left the house I thought it was indeed strange that the television and VCR had been melted by the intense heat yet the plastic prayer cards survived.

I came to the conclusion after the fire at Connie's house that my psychic awareness had reawakened. Of course, I did not know what visions were yet to come. I thanked God there were no messages during that one year period, because my emotional, physical and mental energies needed balance and rest.

I did receive a call from my friend Frank Castelluccio, saying that his mother, Anna, needed open heart surgery and he wanted to know from me what the outcome would be. I told him that the surgery would go well and his mother would be fine.

Anna Castelluccio came through her surgery like a champ. In this case, I was grateful that my gift of sight was back. I realized that this ability, even though it brought painful truths, still helped many people. I sincerely wanted to be of assistance, I just did not know where to start.

My journey began by assisting my friends. As they called me asking for guidance I received messages from the Universe in various ways. They came through my inner voice, visions and through spirit guides, a knowing that comes without explanation.

One of the calls I received was from a despondent friend who was worried about his finances. In fact, he wanted to die because he was facing bankruptcy. As the reading I gave unfolded, I was advised by the Universe that his finances would completely turn around after filing bankruptcy. I was told that his new business venture in mid-1990 would manifest endless amounts of money.

I advised him to declare bankruptcy; then later, if he chose, he could repay the debts. Today he owns a successful product that appears on national television.

I changed my usual route to work on the morning of March 12. I got off the Verranzano Bridge at the first exit and made a right turn onto 86th Street. At 14th Avenue and 86th Street I stopped for a red light. On the left hand side of the street was Scarpaci Funeral Home. As I waited for the light to change I envisioned the funeral home draped in black and I realized Mr. Scarpaci would be passing soon.

His daughter Lena and I were good friends. Lena was a delight. She could make a sour person laugh. Our conversations were usually full of jokes and laughter. Unfortunately, her next call to me was to announce her father's passing.

After Mr. Scarpaci's death, once again my old fear set in and with it my strong recollection of the harsh condemnation of the Catholic priest who said, "Your blood runs cold like a vampire." I had always assumed this superstitious man had meant that my ability to see death approaching was an unnatural or evil gift.

On the morning of April 11, 1989, as I was driving to work I heard my mother's voice in my head. "Go visit Grandpa."

"No," I answered.

"Please, go visit Grandpa," she repeated.

"Mom, I really can't deal with this again."

Once again she asked, "Please, go visit Grandpa."

I continued my drive and parked in front of my business. However, my mother's voice came again, this time more insistent. "Go visit Grandpa."

"Okay, Mom," I said out loud.

I went into the store and told my employees that I was going to visit my grandparents. As I entered the downstairs hallway, I dreaded my next steps. I knew that I would see Great-Grandma Lily waiting for me. I took a deep breath and started up the stairs. There were no words exchanged between us as I passed her, a gentle apparition with a knowing smile.

My grandmother was sitting at the dining room table and was happy to see me. I rarely visited them after my mother passed, but there were daily telephone calls. The simple fact was I avoided them because it was too difficult for me to come to their building where I was forced to pass Mom's former apartment on the first floor.

"My favorite grandson is here," Grandma said smiling.

"Hi Grandma, how are you doing?"

"Is there anything wrong?" she asked.

"No, Grandma."

She looked at me strangely, "Are you sure?"

"Grandma, would I tell you a lie?"

"Not my favorite grandson. Would you like coffee? How about toast and eggs?"

"No thank you Grandma, I have to go back to work, but I wanted to come visit you and Grandpa."

"Grandpa's in the bedroom, he has a cold."

Grandpa looked so thin and drawn lying in bed that I was shaken. I spoke very loudly and called out, "Grandpa."

There was no reply. Once again I heard my mother's voice,

"Shave Grandpa."

"I don't want to," I protested.

"Please, shave Grandpa," she pleaded.

"No."

I stayed with my grandpa for a while, then I returned to the dining room. The coffee cups were already on the table and I could smell buttered toast.

"Grandma, I really can't stay very long."

However, I lingered long enough for coffee and toast. As I was driving back to the store, Mom's voice insisted, "Please, go back and shave Grandpa. And cut his nails," she added.

"I'll shave him, but I'm not cutting Grandpa's nails."

I guess that was my mother's way of winning. She knew that if she made two requests, I would comply with one.

"I'll have Connie cut his nails, but I won't do it. If I cut his nails that means I'm getting him ready to pass."

This may have been my personal superstition but I truly did not want to be part of my grandfather's passing, and I certainly was not ready to cope with death once again. But as I pulled up to the store I knew I could no longer ignore my mother's request. I immediately called my grandmother and told her that I would be back later to shave Grandpa. I also called Connie to tell her that I did not think that Grandpa would live until the next day.

"Ed, please do not say that," Connie pleaded. "Is this one of your visions?"

"Make sure that you visit with him after work," I told her.

Next, I dialed Aunt Carol's number and she agreed to go to my grandparent's house.

When I returned to my grandparents' later I expected to see Great-Grandma Lily in the hall once again, but this time it was empty. I hurried up the stairs and went straight into the bedroom. Grandma was standing near the bed trying to give Grandpa a sip of water. I took out the cordless shaver and shaved him.

"Grandpa looks so much better clean-shaven," Grandma told me.

I washed his face. I noticed that his breathing seemed to be more labored.

Aunt Carol arrived and Connie soon after. I reminded Connie to cut his nails, but still did not tell her about hearing my mother's voice, or about seeing Great-Grandma Lily in the hall. Aunt Carol decided she would call the doctor. He arrived shortly, a young man who was not familiar with our family.

"He should really be in the hospital," he said after a brief examination. "He has pneumonia. I'm going to give him an injection, then I'll try to reach his doctor and have him admitted into the hospital."

"Doctor, before you give my grandfather anything, don't you realize he is dying and the injection or a hospital is not going to do anything for him?" I asked.

"This man has pneumonia," the doctor replied.

"My grandfather has the death rattle," I told him.

He looked at me, I could see he was angry. He replied, "I'm the doctor here."

"I mean no disrespect, but look at my grandfather's feet."

He turned back the blanket and examined my grandfather's feet, then looked at me and said, "Sir, I am terribly sorry, you are correct. This man is dying."

"My grandfather won't last until tomorrow morning," I informed him.

The doctor asked me if I had ever studied medicine and how I was able to make an accurate diagnosis. I responded by telling him that I received information from the Universe.

I stayed with Grandpa for two more hours and said my good-byes. I silently spoke to my mother, telling her how much she was missed and that I knew Grandpa would be with her before morning. And once again, I needed to remind her that when my turn came not to forget to be there for me.

The next morning the phone rang at 7:30. I was asked to hurry to my grandparents' house because Grandpa did not look well and his breathing was very shallow. When I arrived, my grandfather had already passed away.

As I later thought of my grandfather with fondness and love, I realized that he had had more time on earth than many people. He was 100 when he passed into God's White Light.

By this time my immediate family was aware of my psychic gift. After my grandfather's passing I decided to tell them about hearing my mother's voice and seeing Great-Grandma Lily in the hallway. I had refrained from talking about my clairvoyance because I was afraid of ridicule, but surprisingly, they accepted my visions as fact.

Chapter 17

A New Path

My friend Aggie had visited George, a psychic-channeler and prominent medium. When she returned from her session with him she was excited and told a mutual friend about her experience. Intrigued, we scheduled an appointment. Like most people about to visit a psychic, I was excited and hoped I would not be disappointed. I didn't know that this event would change the path of my life.

When I arrived, there were about twenty people sitting on folding chairs in a long, narrow room. I sat down next to Aggie. As George began his readings he gave people information about their loved ones and explained how they passed over. He was three chairs away from where I was sitting, when a spirit child came to me and spoke.

"My name is Eric," the child said. "I died in a car crash."

Meanwhile, George was speaking to Eric's parents about their teenage son, telling them that he was athletic. "He was here a moment ago, where did he go?" George asked.

Of course, the boy had slipped away to speak to me.

"Oh, here he is." George said. "His name begins with an E."

"His name is Eric," I whispered to Aggie. "He died in an automobile accident."

"How do you know?" Aggie asked.

"Because he just told me."

I had no sooner said these words when, George said, "His name is Eric. He died in a car accident."

His parents, who were present in the room, began to cry. When it was my turn for George to speak to me, I trusted him because Eric's appearance had proved his reliability. I still did not believe wholly in my own psychic powers. He did not know that Aggie and I were together.

He told me my mother's name was Mary and that she said hello to me.

My dad came next through George and apologized for teasing me when I was a child. As George spoke my father's words, I could feel myself reacting with the same old anger. I realized I still had not forgiven him and I had to work on my hostile feelings. It wasn't too much later that I reached a point in my life where I did forgive my father, allowing love and respect to come to the front.

That day in the room with George, something powerful stirred in me. It was so reassuring to know that there was another person who also spoke to spirits. And what's more, George didn't fear delivering his profound messages. As I watched each face in the room glow from his reassuring words, I realized how much comfort he gave to the bereaved group. Through him they were linked to their loved ones. My own doorway to a new path was now fully opened.

On my new path, a remarkable psychic, Shoshana, through her consultations with me and her coaching, opened a much broader spiritual vista for me to contemplate. Over the period of a year, with her inspiration I learned to trust the messages that came to me from the other world, in which God's Light is a bright beacon.

As my year working with Shoshana progressed, I could sense a weight being lifted from my heart. It was as if I were stripped naked, then clothed with a new understanding that we are all mirror reflections of one another. It is important to understand this concept because when another person is in pain, he may project his pain onto you.

Chapter 18

Sweet Spirit

On the thirty-second anniversary of my father's death, June 16, 1992, I began public readings. One of my first readings was for a man named John. The woman from the spirit world who came forward to communicate with John was a sweet, gentle soul. But I was confused at first because I saw her as a photograph negative, then I realized that she was African-American.

I informed John that she had taken care of him when he was a child during a period while he was ill. John became upset and said, "I do not believe you."

I thanked the spirit for coming, but she insisted that I give John a final message.

She said, "Tell him my only son was found hanged."

John's eyes flew open; shock flooded his face. "I will never doubt again," John said. "What she said is absolutely true. This woman was my nanny and I loved her dearly."

Connections with souls who have gone to the other side often occurred in surprising circumstances. One evening I was sitting in a restaurant with a friend Steve, when a young man came to our table.

"I'm sorry to disturb you, but I'm here in New York on business and I'm not familiar with this area. Can you tell me how to get to Lincoln Center?"

After giving him the directions to Lincoln Center he put out his hand. "My name is Tom," he said.

As I shook his hand, my thumb rested on top of a diamond that was set in his ring. Suddenly I experienced a strange sensation as the right side of my mouth drooped as if an invisible hand had pulled it downward. I wiped my lower lip as I spoke. Afflicted with this odd facial deformity, I began telling the young man about his grandfather, who was the original owner of the ring.

"What you are doing with your lip is amazing," Tom said. "My grandfather used to look like that."

I apologized for my expression. I couldn't explain it.

"If you do not mind, would you continue?" Tom asked.

"Whatever wrong your grandfather did to your family, he is truly sorry," I told him. "When he became crippled he blamed your father, and he wanted to make your whole family suffer. He made your life miserable."

Tom nodded in acknowledgment, then said that he loved his grandfather and he was grateful that he was apologizing. "Does he know how much I love him?" Tom asked.

"Tom, he says he loves you, too."

Chapter 19

The Priest

As I grew more confident of my abilities, I became capable of manifesting or bringing goodness to myself, but I was still unable to let go of a fear. Even though I worked with Shoshana and many other wonderful teachers, I was still afraid of the intuitive knowledge that I'd possessed since I was a baby. I knew that I was able to see into the past, present and future and to foresee illness, death and even the beginning of a new life. In the business world I manifested what I needed to provide for my family. However, in the spiritual realm, I was still influenced by the condemnatory words of the Catholic priest who had cursed me years ago with his assertion that my blood ran cold. It took another priest to free me and teach me that the work I did helped others calm their fears of the unknown. From that priest, I also accepted his assurance that I was destined to help ease the shattering loss and pain that came to people when someone special they loved died.

I was with a friend, Ralph, having a drink one night when a stranger approached me.

"I was told you were a psychic," he said. "And I hope you don't mind the interruption, but I need your help."

"What is your question?" I asked.

"If I tell you my question, then you'll know what the answer is."

"May I feel your vibrations?" I asked. I placed my forefinger and index finger in the center of his palm. "I can only tell you what I hear," I told him. "You can do God's work anywhere."

"What do you mean?" he asked, his face expressionless.

"Excuse me, Father," I said. "In your office, directly in front of your desk, is a large wooden cross. You just left your position with the Church. You were a hierarch in the Roman Catholic Church."

He looked at me and smiled. "You are absolutely correct," he said.

I asked if he would mind if I turned the tables and asked him a question. I told him the story of the priest who had compared me to a vampire.

"Your blood does not run cold," he assured me, smiling. "You're a very gifted man. Don't ever stop sharing your wonderful gift. It comes from God for you to give to the world."

Strangely, it was a priest who embedded the nails of fear in my heart and another who pulled them out and helped soothe the pain. The summer of 1993 was when I finally lost all fear of my special foresight and continued my exploration into the world of the paranormal.

Chapter 20

Past Lives

It wasn't very long after my meeting with the second priest that I decided to educate myself about past life regression. I made an appointment to be hypnotized by Dr. George Bien. When I arrived at Dr. Bien's office, I was a little apprehensive, wondering if I could be hypnotized. The first time we shook hands I could feel that he was warm and honest. He escorted me into his hypnotherapy room which was equipped with recording gear. He explained that the recording instruments would chronicle the session so that I would lose nothing that was spoken in the session. I was seated in a comfortable chair when the session began. Dr. Bien spoke very softly. As he talked, his voice resonated deeply in my being. He was a kind and perceptive man.

"Now, I want you to imagine that you are standing inside the door to your home and that you are opening the door," he said. "Imagine that the door opens into a long tunnel and there is a light at the end. I am going to count from twenty backwards to one. I want you to imagine that with each number I speak, you are moving down through the tunnel toward the light. I want you to imagine that you are moving toward the light and back through time to a lifetime you lived previous to this one. And, when I reach the number 'one' you will step from the tunnel into the light, into that previous lifetime."

As he spoke, I felt myself totally relax. I could hear myself answering his questions, yet I felt disconnected from the outside world. When the session was over, Dr. Bien said that it was a profound experience for him. He told me that at times I did not speak, but the expressions on my face, laughter and tears were wonderful to watch. He handed me my tape and I thanked him.

As I got back into my car, I felt as if the session had only lasted for ten minutes. When I looked at the clock on the dashboard I was astonished to see that it was an hour and half later.

I took the cassette and placed it into the tape deck. As I heard myself speak during the session I listened in disbelief. I was describing a past life in a monastery, disclosing details as to what I was wearing. In my hypnotic state I recognized another person from that lifetime as someone who, like me, lived in the present. I saw that person among a group of people who were working in a field of vegetables. Actually, I did not recognize his face, because it was different from the face he wore in present-day life. But I recognized him by his spiritual essence.

Toward the end of the tape, Dr. Bien had asked me to go back to the beginning of time. He questioned where I was and what I was looking at. I told him that I could see

Earth as if from a great distance, from a location that I thought was the universal realm.

After listening to the taped session I was still skeptical and doubted if I could be hypnotized. I decided to go to another hypnotist, and it was from him, Bob, that I learned that I was a suitable subject for hypnotherapy. As a result of this interview, I was convinced that my regression experiment truly represented another life I had led.

Later, I couldn't help but recall Barbra Streisand singing, "On a clear day, rise and look around you and see who you are …"

I have come to understand that we are far more than we think we are. We are spiritual Kings and Queens, Masters of the Universe, Children of God. Death is simply another version of who we are. If we can truly understand this, imagine what we could do with our lives? Unshackled from the bonds of mortality, we could act and behave as if our souls were truly unlimited, giving us the power that Edna St. Vincent Millay described so superbly in her remarkable poem, *Renascence*: "The soul can split the sky in two, and let the face of God shine through."

It is the desire to pierce the darkness that shrouds the idea of death which has prompted you, the reader, to purchase this book and seek personal answers for the puzzle of dying — answers which may illuminate your ignorance of who you are, why you are here and whether or not you and your loved ones have a destiny loftier than the grave.

I have read much about death and the mystery of the soul, and one of the spiritual masters I like is Ravi Ravindra, a celebrated professor of physics at Dalhousie University in Halifax, Nova Scotia. He has addressed the perennial question about the veil that shields the spirit, by writing about the mystery of us:

.,c ourselves are as mysterious as the kingdom and .iiay hold the keys to it. If we can open the doors to the interior castle, the king might come and sit on the throne."

It is to this interior castle, dear reader, that I wish to lead you. I believe my experience with visitors from the "other side" has led me to understand that the only way to God is self-knowing, dying to outer self, and being born to a deeper inner self.

"Spiritual becoming is the path," Ravindra says, "to the interior castle which searchers of the self eventually find. It is another name for the Divine Consciousness, which one may only recognize when he penetrates the nature of his own soul."

Ravindra adds that it is only when we search deeper down that there is the possibility of increased under-standing: "Only in a state of collectedness, composure, openness, and alertness can we know anything objectively. In all other states, our perceiving apparatus is out of tune and introduces its own noise arising out of internal or external distractions and affliction. Nothing we decipher in these dispersed states is ultimately trustworthy."

Finding one's way into this purified state of being to which Ravindra alludes, certainly does not happen overnight. But that should never be an excuse to put off the self-discovery that leads to being an expanded human — a person who can accept both the grandness and the humility that goes with understanding that death is but another step closer to God. God from whom we received the breath of life, just as we give it up when we die and are transformed — back to God.

I should make an important point here: There are many psychics who, unfortunately, are cynical and dishonest about the revelations they make. In my own case, I made an investigation of how other readers handled themselves and how they delivered their messages. I visited about twenty psychic readers in the New York area. According to my estimate, only ten percent were totally accurate. However, I really was not assessing their accuracy rate; instead, I was examining their techniques and their honesty. I learned that each psychic must develop his own way of expressing candor, love, and most of all, must understand his clients' fears. Today, it is so easy to pick up the phone and dial a psychic. In fact, to work as a telephone psychic, all you need is a deck of tarot cards. I am not inferring that phone psychics don't have valuable insights. There are some truly gifted psychics working the phones, but there are others whose sense of responsibility to a bereaved person seeking solace is highly questionable.

As part of learning to say good-bye to loved ones and accepting that their destiny, and yours, when the time comes, is a new life, I have presented stories of my personal encounters with men and women who desperately wish to be able to believe that their loved ones who have passed over are safe and happy in a brighter dimension. All of us crave proof of life hereafter. Yet the proof is all around us, the evidence of which comes to us in the form of miracles, prayers that are answered, and testimony and recitations of messages from beyond through sensitives, like me, who have struggled to accept their gift as conduits, channels, contacts, for the voices from beyond.

The problem for the survivor who has lost a beloved is one of what and whom to believe. Whose interpretation of death should he or she, suffering the pain of loss, believe in? It is easy for the pragmatists to say life ends at the grave, because there is no substantive evidence that it goes on.

It takes far more courage, and more personal inspiration, to stretch the soul to embrace an unseen future that promises a reunion of the spirit with its origin–maker — God.

And that is why I have devoted this book to tell you my story of spiritual awakening and my experiences with those whose own stories of seeking contact with loved ones passed on help us to have faith in God, which in turn gives us peace and a sense of our divine destiny.

Despite my deepening conviction that I had a gift of seeing that should be shared with others searching for answers about dying, it took me more than a year to decide whether I was worthy of becoming an ordained minister. It was Sandy Bellamy, one of the directors of Universal Brotherhood who helped me make my decision, as well as the son of a dear friend. Part of my dilemma was that I did not want to change my Roman Catholic beliefs, and so I decided to become affiliated with an interfaith ministry. The deciding factor in my decision was that as part of my counseling and healing work, sometimes my clients asked me to perform marriage ceremonies.

Weddings brought me the greatest joy in my helping role, because there was so much love exchanged during a wedding ceremony. Of course, along with the joy in my new designation, there was also sadness. There were those times when I was called on to visit someone who was ill or when a family member requested that I help a loved one pass over.

It was a boy who became the catalyst for my decision to become an ordained minister.

I received a phone call informing me that Damion, the son of a friend of mine, had been gravely injured in an automobile accident which had instantly taken his father's life.

Rafaela, my friend and Damion's mother, requested that I come to the hospital and perform a healing on Damion. I asked my friends Aggie and Bob to accompany me. As we drove to the hospital in New Jersey, we prayed for Damion.

When we arrived, we were escorted into the intensive care unit. Damion lay in a bed at the far left side of the room. At first it appeared to us that Damion did not have a mark on his body from the accident. I had not seen the left side of his head yet, but I understood it had been crushed in the accident.

There was one particular monitor in the intensive care unit that measured Damion's brain waves. We quickly discovered that the machine was registering activity far above normal. If it remained at the high ranges, Damion would be considered to be brain dead.

As the three of us began our healing ritual, the monitor dropped to a safe level. The healing work we were doing consisted of transmitting an energy from a higher source of power to Damion. There is a wide range of healing techniques to help the injured, including prayer. All of them invoke the help of God. We knew that we were merely the conduits drawing down the higher source of power that we directed to Damion.

A nurse, who stood behind us observing our actions, answered the question of a young doctor who observed, "Do you see the level of the monitor? What are they doing?"

"Quiet," she said. "They are praying."

When we completed our healing and prayers, we joined Damion's mother, Rafaela, in the family waiting room. She was distraught, not only over the death of her husband, but the balance between life and death in which her son hovered.

"Ed, what do you think?" Rafaela asked.

"Rafaela, this is Damion's choice," I said. "He can choose to stay on earthplane or walk into God's White Light."

"With Fred gone, I cannot lose my son, too," she told me and began sobbing.

We stayed with Rafaela for a while before we returned to the intensive care unit to pray again, before leaving for New York. During our second visit, the brain activity monitor indicated a dangerous level in Damion's condition. This time, as we prayed and performed a healing ritual, there was no encouraging movement of the needle.

The next afternoon, I received a call from Rafaela begging me to come back and pray for Damion. Rafaela acknowledged to me that the doctors had warned her there was no hope for her son. But Aggie, Bob and I drove to the hospital once again and walked into Damion's room. Even though his physical body was lying in the bed, I could see his etheric body standing near the bed holding on to a saintly female figure. I knew then that Damion was trying to make the decision of whether to go with the Heavenly Mother or stay on earthplane with his loved ones.

I spoke to the etheric Damion and said, "It is your choice. Your mom and sisters will be fine."

Neither Bob, Aggie nor I did a healing. We simply prayed for Damion to make his own choice. When I left the room, once again his mother asked me, "Ed, what do you think?"

"Rafaela, I can only tell you what I saw. Damion was with the Blessed Mother. He has to make his own choice. It is a tough one because he loves you very dearly. Rafaela, sometimes we can hold our loved ones earthbound because of the great love we feel for them."

"I know," she said.

"If you understand that, then you must tell Damion that it's all right to go, so he can feel less earthbound by your love."

I was not called by Damion's family the next evening. Instead, a Roman Catholic healing priest was asked to visit him. When he went into Damion's room he asked to be alone with the boy. When he came from the room to talk with the family, he asked them to stop praying and promised that he would take over their prayers. He said the family's prayers were preventing Damion from making his final decision.

Aggie, Bob and I went to see Damion one more time. Once again, I saw that he was talking with the Blessed Mother. All he needed from his earth mother was her unconditional love and her permission for him to leave.

Damion passed over the next day. He walked into the Kingdom of the Angels, hand in hand with the Blessed Mother to meet his father on the other side.

Many times I've seen a loved one ready to depart held back by the well-intentioned prayers of relatives. During each of my visits with Damion I was allowed to spend only a limited amount of time in his hospital room. However, if I had been an ordained minister I would have been able to stay longer with Damion to help ease his way into the hereafter sooner.

In a very real sense, it was Damion who inspired my decision to become ordained.

Chapter 21

Psychics and Reading Tools

Many people have asked me how to determine whether a psychic is genuine. While many people claim to be "psychic," usually they are only highly intuitive or experience occasional ESP. In the chapter entitled Past Lives, I mentioned briefly that there are numerous "telephone psychics" who are more interested in fees than in the quality of their services. The following information will help readers to make intelligent choices as to the genuineness of the psychic they propose to use.

People with psychic abilities usually acquire their talent in one of two ways: they are either born with them or they appear when they are faced with life-threatening traumas. If a person is born with psychic ability, he begins to manifest his talents in early childhood.

Responsible psychics do not encourage their clients to return for regular or frequent readings, because they don't want them to depend on the readings to make decisions. Instead, readings should be used as one of many tools to facilitate inner growth.

Methods of readings vary with the psychic's preferred style. There are many different types of tools that can be used during a reading. Psychics may use a combination of tarot cards, crystal balls, palmistry, tea leaves and photographs.

If a so-called psychic claims that you have barriers in your life such as money or relationship problems, or difficulties with work and she can remove them by using a ritual or prayer for a large sum of money, I suggest that you refuse. Such a person would be taking advantage of you. Give your trust and faith to God and place your difficulties in his hands. Any person claiming to be clairvoyant and putting a high price on his or her disclosures should be avoided.

One example of fraud came to my attention when a young woman phoned me. I had given her a reading two weeks before her call. She explained she needed to see me immediately because another reader insisted that she could bring the woman's ex-boyfriend back for $5,000. I told her it was not necessary for her to see me and certainly not give the reader one red cent. I hope she took my advice.

I think it is a wonderful experience to have a consultation with a psychic. However, you must always remember to be discerning and discard any information or advice that you do not think is appropriate. If a psychic somehow frightens you, do not carry the burden of her words. Everything you are told does not mean that it will come to full fruition.

I received a phone call from another young woman, named Jennifer, who told me that she had just left a reader's home. This reader had told her that her mother was going to die within the next few weeks. Jennifer was so frantic that I arranged an appointment with her immediately.

When Jennifer arrived she was still shaken from the psychic's words. I told Jennifer that it was not her mother's time, and that she would not be dying within the next few weeks. Jennifer asked me if I were certain of this, and I assured her that I was positive the other reader was wrong and her mother was not failing in any way.

As Jennifer and I continued talking, she calmed down. This happened about a year ago and Jennifer's mother is still with us.

When you make arrangements for a reader, you should be aware that an honest psychic will establish the fee before the reading and ask for nothing beyond this. At one time I could not understand why there had to be an exchange of money for the messages that came to me so easily. Now, I understand that one of the primary reasons for exchanging money is so that you hold no collective karma. The exchange of money is similar to the exchange of energy. Paying a fee also gives the client an incentive to appreciate and to listen closely to the messages that are delivered.

Chapter 22

Listen to the Children

The insights from beyond that come to little children can be the most profound, joyful and fearless. I consider it a privilege to listen and talk to them

My friend Joni has two grandchildren: Gianna, four, and Vincent, one. One day, their mother, Jeannine, was holding Vincent in her arms while Gianna was walking alongside of her, when they were detained by a neighbor who wanted to chat briefly with Jeannine. Gianna knew that she wasn't allowed to cross the street by herself, but she was impatient about the delay and excited about visiting her grandparents. While Jeannine and the neighbor talked, Gianna decided that she would make the journey across the street on her own.

As she dashed suddenly across the street, she was hit by a car and tossed in the air. When her frantic mother reached her, Gianna was in shock, but she did not have a scratch on her body, nor did she suffer any broken bones. Taken to the doctor immediately, she kept repeating, "When I got hit by the car the angels caught me, that's why I wasn't hurt."

Gianna never mentioned the angels again until four years later when she and her brother, Vincent, were in the car with their grandfather. Their grandfather was parking his car and Vincent thought the car was stopped and pushed open the door to get out. Vincent's grandfather yelled at him for opening up the door and warned him he could get hurt.

"Vincent, you have to be careful," Gianna scolded her brother. "When I crossed the street by myself, I got hit by a car, but the angels caught me and that's why I didn't get hurt."

When Vincent was ten months old, his great-grandfather "Poppy" passed away. On the great-grandfather's anniversary, Vincent and his family went to the grave to place flowers. On the way to the cemetery, their grandmother, Joni, explained to Vincent that Poppy was in heaven.

"No, he's not," Vincent replied. "He's not in heaven. He is in the attic."

"What does Poppy do in the attic?" Joni asked.

"He is watching over Great-Grandma, so she doesn't fall and doesn't burn the pots."

"How do you know?" Joni asked.

"Because he told me," Vincent replied. "He laughs when I come up the stairs." Then Vincent went on to say, "Your uncle is in the attic, too. Poppy is with your uncle."

"Which uncle" Joni asked.

"Great-Grandma's brother," Vincent told her. "I don't know his name, but they are up there having a good time."

The messages from the mouths of her small grandchildren helped their great-grandmother believe in the ultimate reunion of loved ones.

✥✥✥✥✥

The following story about an infant saved by an angel has an unusual twist, as you will see. It was contributed by Pamela Penrose of Portland, Oregon, and describes her harrowing escape from death when she was four months old. I include the story here with her permission.

Saved by an Angel

Seven-year-old Pamela Penrose, who lived with her parents and brothers and sisters in Artesia, California, crawled into her bed and pulled the blankets under her chin. She was hopeful, as she cuddled against her pillow, that she would not have one of the frightening dreams that often woke her with a rapidly beating heart and a clutching fear that she would die. Often she threw her covers aside and bolted to the closet in her room and hid behind her clothes that hung from the pole suspended between the walls. There she would stay in a dark corner haunted by her nightmare and shivering with terror until she worked up the courage to run into the living room and switch on the TV. With the volume turned low, she watched the comforting images on the screen until she fell into an exhausted sleep on the couch, or until the morning light chased away the shadows.

One Friday night in May, 1959, despite her vague apprehension about a nightmare visitation, she fell into a deep, peaceful sleep until the image of herself as an infant cuddling in a bassinet on the rear seat of her father's car came into her mind. Usually, when a terrifying dream was taking shape in her consciousness, she would have a warning that it was going to be bad and the warning was always accompanied by a desperate, sinking feeling. But in her dreaming mind the picture of herself, a dark-haired little baby with rosy cheeks, certainly no older than four months, assured her there was nothing to fear.

Even though her father, behind the wheel of the car, was driving erratically and loudly berating her mother — pounding her with his brutal voice and drawing silent tears — the baby in the bassinet seemed undisturbed. There was no question in that portion of Pam's mind which was monitoring her dream, that the infant in the back seat was herself, seven years earlier

She thought it strange, though, that the baby was not screaming with fright from her father's awful shouting anger and his maniacal driving. Now, suddenly, he whipped the steering wheel in a sharp turn that drew screeching protest from the tires as the car lurched to the right.

That was the moment when the right rear door, behind her mother's front passenger seat, flew open and the infant Pam was wrenched from her bassinet and hurled out the yawning door.

For an instant, Pam's mother turned in her seat and watched with horrified eyes as her infant daughter flew from her safe perch on the back seat through the open space of the flung-out door. Pam's tiny body made an arc, then, with a thump, struck the hood of a truck trailing slightly behind the Penrose's car in the outside right lane. After striking the pickup, the baby's body disappeared, falling beneath the speeding truck.

It was the terrible, crumpled expression on her mother's face that touched seven-year-old Pam's heart as she saw her mother dissolve into tears and shake as she screamed at her husband to stop the car. It was in that same briefest of moments, after baby Pam collided with the hood of the pickup, that the dreaming Pam witnessed what she thought was a blue cloud of smoke appear in the open rear door frame, then vanish like a sudden wind. She would never forget, as the cloud passed, the sense of marvelous peace that stole through her body and imparted to her the unquestionable knowledge that baby Pam was safe, enfolded protectively in the arms of an angel!

Baby Pam was alive and safe! She did not die under the wheels of the pickup truck. Dreaming Pam knew, as a solemn, incontrovertible truth, that nothing would change. She as a baby had been saved from death by an angel. With a huge sigh and a warm feeling in her heart, Pam fell into a dreamless sleep.

It was at breakfast the next morning that Pam's mother made a startling announcement. Just the two of them, Pam and her mother, Dione, sat across from each other at the table. Pam had eaten her oatmeal and an orange, while her mother lingered over her coffee.

From the moment she had seated herself after serving her daughter's breakfast, Dione had seemed strangely quiet, perturbed, with her brow wrinkled as if she were searching for the right words to convey a special thought.

Finally, she said, "I think you are old enough for me to tell you about something that happened when you were a baby."

Pam looked at her mother sharply. What could her mother have to say to her that required a certain maturity on Pam's part to understand? She waited while her mother collected her thoughts and, choosing her words carefully, said, "When you were little, oh, about four months old, you were in the car with your dad and me when he took a sharp turn. You flew out of your bassinet on the back seat and tumbled out of the rear door, which had popped open. It must not have been closed all the way.

"Anyway, you bounced off a pickup truck in the next lane and fell beneath the wheels. It all happened so fast that there was nothing I could do. I thought I'd go crazy. Anyway, the truck passed over you. Your face was scraped but, miraculously, except for cuts on your face, you were not injured. The police came and called an ambulance. Doctors examined you at the hospital and everybody said it was a miracle you were alive. I thanked God for saving you. It was a miracle. Whenever you get sick or overtired, you can see the tiny scars on your face. They show up then!"

Pam had been holding her tongue, incredulous that her mother somehow knew about her dream. She had not whispered a word about it. She never told her parents, or anybody, about any of her dreams. Even when they were horrible and frightening, she kept them to herself.

Furious with her mother, she shouted, "You're lying to me! Why would you lie to me?"

Dione Penrose sat back in her chair as if she had been struck by her daughter.

"Why would I lie to you?" she asked, leaning forward across the table and taking Pam's small hands in hers.

Confused, and ashamed that she had screamed at her mother, Pam mumbled, "I don't know. Why did you tell me now? I mean, why today?"

"I don't know," Dione said. "It just seemed like the proper time. I had no idea you'd be so upset."

Later, in her room, convinced that her mother's revelation was a strange coincidence, Pam suddenly felt a sense of deep peace settle over her and, although no voice came into her mind to explain the understanding that flowed into her like a soft and gentle whisper, she knew in her heart that the source of her wisdom was the same angelic visitor who had clasped her infant body in a protective embrace to save her life when she was four months old.

Chapter 23

Phone Consultation

There are many people who cannot travel to the New York area, but call me for phone readings. Here is a story from a woman who reached me from California.

Mon Cheri

The woman's name was Lisa and she spoke with a French accent. At first, I couldn't understand her words on the phone, because she was crying as if her heart were broken.

"My Francis died," she sobbed over and over.

I learned that Francis, her lover, had passed over during the night.

"Do you think you can reach him?" Lisa asked. "Or is it too soon?"

I asked Lisa to calm herself while I communicated

with Francis. Summoning him was almost like picking up a telephone and dialing a number, because he answered me immediately.

"Lisa," I said after conversing with Francis, "Francis just told me that he passed over very quickly. He had a heart attack, and he did not bleed to death."

"When the paramedics picked up his body they told me that they believed he bled to death after he fell," Lisa exclaimed. "They told me he must have suffered for the remainder of the night."

"No," I said. "He explained to me that when he fell he hit his head on the floor. That is where all the blood came from."

Francis asked me to tell his grieving Lisa that even though he did not use the word "love" often to her, he loved and cherished her very dearly.

"He said that he called you *Mon Cheri.*"

"Is he angry with me?" Lisa asked. She was referring to an argument the night before he died, after which Francis returned to his own apartment. There he fell to floor when he was struck by the heart seizure. The impact of the fall opened his head and he bled profusely. The two would not have had their disagreement, Lisa said, if only he had told her that he dearly loved her.

I assured her that he was not angry with her and gave her his request that she tell his family that he was with his grandmother.

Just as the communication with Francis was spontaneous and the connection made quickly, our conversation ended just as abruptly.

Lisa called me about two weeks later to inform me that an autopsy revealed that Francis had certainly died from a heart attack, and that he had not bled to death. She was relieved that his passing occurred quickly with little pain. And she thanked me for restoring her peace of mind and convincing her, through Francis, that he had loved her with all his heart.

The Last Dance

I received a call early one morning.

"I am so sorry to bother you at eight in the morning. My name is Roe, I got your number from my friend, Betty, who came to you for a reading."

As my caller rambled on, I had to tell her to slow down.

Making a deliberate attempt to be more collected, Roe said, "I need to know that he is all right. He died from AIDS."

"Roe, who passed over?" I asked.

"My brother," she answered.

"Are you saying that you are afraid he did not make it to God's White Light because he died from this particular disease?"

"Well, yes," was Roe's reply. "Can you help me? I need to know that Tom's okay."

"Roe," I began, "although he lived a different lifestyle, that doesn't mean he didn't pass over into the heavenly realm."

I asked Roe to hold on one moment while I communicated with her brother Tom.

"Roe, your brother tells me that he danced his way to the other side. He is showing me a pair of tap shoes, and tells me that you and he were a dance team when you were younger."

I could hear her crying.

"Tom says that you do not have to worry about him," I went on. "He is out of pain. And, when it's your time to pass over, he will be waiting for one last dance."

She was sobbing after hearing her brother's assurances from me. I waited for her to calm down before I continued, "Your brother would like to thank you for being there and making his last days on the earthplane comfortable."

I never was able to meet Roe in person.

Plaid Shirt

My friend Steve and I were working together on a children's spiritual book. After he'd been with me for about an hour, he asked if he could use my telephone to call his mother who lived in another state. He had been unable to reach his family for the past two days.

After he dialed, I heard him say, "Oh hi, Uncle Gary. Where have you been for the past couple of days?"

To his uncle's reply, I heard Steve say, "Does anyone know where he is?" Then he asked to speak with his mother. After a few minutes I heard him exclaim, "Oh Mama, that's terrible."

When Steve completed his phone call, my curiosity was aroused. He told me that a friend of his family, Ron, was missing and Steve's mother was greatly concerned because he had left a suitcase, presumably with clothes in it, in Steve's mother's garage with her permission.

Almost immediately I had a vision of the missing man, who was wearing a plaid shirt and brown pants. Next I saw a car that appeared to be parked near two tall oil rigs and an adjacent body of water. I warned Steve that I saw there were drugs in Ron's suitcase which he had left behind.

"What do you think happened to Ron?" Steve asked.

"I believe this man was murdered," I said.

At this point, Steve asked if I would mind if he used my phone again.

"I need to call my mother back," he said.

Steve asked his mother whether Ron had been wearing a plaid shirt and brown pants when he disappeared, and he asked for confirmation that Ron had left a suitcase in her garage.

His mother verified the accuracy of my impression about Ron's clothes but told her son that a few days before Ron was presumed missing, he had returned long enough to retrieve the suitcase from the garage and take it with him

"Was his car found in an area near oil wells?" Steve asked.

"Yes," she answered.

"Mama," he said, "do you know that he might have had drugs in that suitcase?"

"Do you think if I had known there were drugs in the suitcase that I would have given him permission to leave it here?"

A few days later she called Steve to tell him that the police believed drugs certainly were a probable factor in Ron's disappearance. Unfortunately, five years after Steve learned about his missing friend, Ron still had not communicated with either Steve or his mother.

Chapter 24

Institute of
Creative Healing

A while back, I was introduced by my friend Shelly to Helene, the founder of the Institute of Creative Healing, an organization that led me further down my life path.

Not long after I met Helene, she invited me to be the evening keynote speaker for a bereavement group, a gathering of people who were interested in peeking beyond the veil. Most of the members of the group had lost children, husbands or wives. When I arrived there were approximately thirty people in the room. As I looked at each person's face I murmured the Lord's Prayer and asked God for the strength to give each of them exactly what he or she needed to hear. I also asked God to banish my old fears so that I could work freely.

I remembered the priest who told me that my gift of sight came from God. That night, as I brought forth each person's loved one, there were tears of joy and sadness.

The Rose

One of the members with whom I worked at the center was named Ed. Before I began, Ed asked to speak with me for a moment alone.

He said, "I need to tell you that I am not a believer."

"That is fine," I responded. "I am not here to make you a believer." I thanked him for his honesty.

As we entered the room I looked at the other faces. I wondered if I could help them. I took in three deep breaths and put my fears aside. Then, I spoke to each person individually. When I came to Ed, the nonbeliever, I stopped for a moment and said, "Your daughter tells me that she is always around you. She hands you a rose every day. She is wearing a green dress."

"I don't know what that means," Ed answered.

I could tell that he still refused to believe. At the end of the evening he thanked me courteously and said, "The others seemed to be quite impressed. But I don't understand what you meant."

"I think in time you will understand," I assured him.

The next day I received a call from Helene, the woman who had invited me to the center.

After she greeted me, she said, "Ed told you that he didn't know what the rose and the green dress meant. But he called, excited and eager to see you again, because he remembered that in the hallway of his home there is a picture on the wall of his daughter in a green dress holding a single rose.

On my next visit to the center, Ed's daughter came forth once again, but out of respect for Ed's privacy, I cannot reveal the information that was given.

Second Hand Shoes

Another client I worked with was Marsha, a sweet senior citizen. Marsha's vibrations could light up a room. She is always eager to help and learn. As I worked with Marsha, her husband, who had passed over seventeen years earlier, came through to speak to her. Strangely, he showed me a pair of old shoes. As I relayed this image, the look on Marsha's face was one of confusion. After a moment of thought she explained that her husband only bought second-hand shoes.

Marsha's husband went on to tell me that there were three celebrations coming up all in the same day.

Marsha smiled. "Yes there are," she answered. "My husband's birthday and our anniversary."

I smiled and felt warmed knowing in advance the nature of the third celebration.

"And the day we first met," Marsha said. "They all come on the same day."

"Your husband tells me that you both loved to dance," I told Marsha.

"Yes we did," she replied. "And I miss him so dearly."

Marsha was pleased with the messages from her husband. She told me that they brought her peace of mind to know that in some form she could still communicate with him.

Whenever I've seen Marsha since our first meeting, I see a pair of dancing shoes in my mind's eye and that is how I know that her husband is with us.

Don't Feel Guilty

I met a woman and her daughter Nancy at the center. They came to see me two months after a tragic loss. The mother was in such pain that I held her hand to comfort her. Then I asked her daughter who had passed over to come forward.

"Your daughter tells you not to feel guilty," I began.

"I do feel guilty," she admitted.

"You did not give her the cancer that she died from," I told her.

Her other daughter, Nancy, who accompanied her to the center, told me some of the details of her sister's illness and death. I turned to Nancy and said, "Your sister has shown me a scapula (a small picture of a saint). You took it from her the day she passed over."

Nancy asked if her sister was upset that she took the scapula.

"No, she is not angry with you," I responded.

"Why did you give the scapula to your aunt?" I asked.

"I gave it to my aunt because she was very sick," Nancy said. "However, from the moment I gave it to her, I wanted to ask for it back, but I felt guilty about being an Indian giver."

"Nancy," I went on. "Your sister said she knows you have a very big heart, but she would like you to have the scapula."

"Do you think I could ask my aunt for it?" Nancy asked.

"Your sister is telling you to ask for it back. She assures me that your aunt will not be angry."

I saw Nancy about two weeks later. She was pleased to show me that she was wearing the scapula and told me that her aunt was happy to return it. Nancy thanked me again for the communication with her sister and told me that her mother's conscience was eased.

The Blinking Light

Petrina was another member of the bereavement group. When it was her turn for her loved one to come forth, I received a message from her son, Freddie. He told me that his mother was a very private person, so I asked her if she would mind meeting at the end of the evening. Then, I could deliver her message without others present. She agreed.

At the end of the evening, Petrina's message was a kiss and a hug from her son, Freddie.

Petrina cried and asked if she could meet with me alone. I agreed.

When I arrived at Petrina's home, the lights blinked. Petrina explained that every time she felt her son's presence they would blink.

I could see Freddie standing by the kitchen sink. While he was alive, this was the place where he and his mother often had their conversations. The most important message Freddie had for his parents was love.

I gave his words to his mother: "It is now time for you to enjoy your life. Life should be lived and enjoyed to the fullest, and sorrow is yesterday's news."

As I related his last words, tears ran down Petrina's face.

"I know that is what my son, Freddie, would want," she told me. "I just can't let go."

When I met his sister, Deena, Freddie told me how he regretted missing a dance with her at her wedding. They were scheduled to dance to the song "My Way."

Deena told me that she had intended to instruct the band to play "My Way" as the last song of the night, but with all of the excitement of the day's festivities, she simply forgot.

Daily Double

Claudia was another woman in the bereavement group. She was struggling to cope with losing her father, Louis, and came to me hoping to receive messages from him. Her father came through with ease.

One of his first messages was, "Don't fence with things."

"That was one of my father's favorite expressions," Claudia told me.

"Your father wants me to tell you that he loves the other side so much, it is better than the daily double."

Claudia explained that this was another one of his infamous expressions.

Claudia then asked about her mother. From the way she posed her question I thought that her mother was in the spirit world. However, as I reached into the spirit world I could not find her.

"Your mother has not passed over." I told Claudia.

"My mother is not dead," she replied. "I want to know if he has a message for her."

Louis talked about his medal that was missing and mentioned that Claudia's mother was always misplacing things.

Claudia chuckled.

Then my hands began to shake. As Claudia noticed this, she explained that her father had Parkinson's disease and his hands used to shake, just like mine.

"Sometimes my physical body takes on the characteristics of the loved one I am working with," I explained to Claudia.

"Your father mentions papers that will be coming to you," I told Claudia. "He tells me that the papers won't be pleasant and you will be going to court."

"Yes, I am waiting for papers to come in the mail," she responded.

"He tells me it will be a slow process, but all will be fine in the end," I assured her.

Louis also told her not to worry about the finances of the business and that she should play more and worry less.

Claudia has since sent me many clients.

Is It Okay?

A sweet-looking woman, twenty-one years old, sat with a group of people. She wanted to speak with her brother who had passed away. As her brother came forth, I could feel a tremendous pressure on the side of my head and I realized that her brother had been shot.

"Your brother tells me that he is not angry at your choice," I said to her.

She looked at me with tears in her eyes and I noticed that she was nervous about what I revealed in front of the group. It was clear that she was reticent about revealing certain personal facts. Her brother knew what was meant by the "choice" she had made. She had chosen a "gay" sexual orientation and wanted her dead brother's approval.

I began to speak to her in a very gentle voice, "Your brother is not judging you. Are you judging yourself?

"Maybe," was her answer.

"If you judge yourself, then how can you expect others not to judge you? All your brother would like is for you to be happy."

She asked again if her brother was certain about his approval.

"Absolutely," was the reply I gave her from him.

"If my brother were still alive he would have judged me harshly," she exclaimed.

"When you are in the spirit world, there is no judging of others." I explained.

Sometimes when I am working with someone and there are other people around, and their loved one gives me a personal message, I try to word it such in a way that only the person in the audience for which it is intended can understand. If she misses the full meaning of the message, I tell her that I will speak to her privately.

Little Larry

I met AnnMarie and Larry at the center eight months after their son Larry Jr. died. The first time I communicated with the younger Larry, I couldn't understand why he would only speak in half sentences, dance away, and return a moment or two later to complete the second half of the sentence. As he relayed his messages in this manner I said to his parents, "I can't understand why he starts to give me a message, goes away for a bit and then comes back to finish."

They explained that this behavior was exactly what their son did while he was on the earthplane.

"He was always on the move, doing three and four things at once. He never sat still," his mother explained. "He was eighteen years old. Even when there was nothing going on, he always had something to do."

One message from Larry Jr. was quite sentimental and touching. It came through just before Christmas of 1996, and young Larry told me that he intended to leave a rocking horse Christmas ornament under the tree as a gift for his mother.

After the holidays, I talked to Larry and AnnMarie and they informed me with happy tears in their eyes that, indeed, under the tree on Christmas Eve they found a rocking horse ornament that seemed to have fallen off the tree.

"Larry Jr. tells me that he loved angel food cake," I told AnnMarie.

"Yes," she replied. "little Larry loved angel food cake."

"This one will have chocolate icing," I told her.

Well, he certainly loved angel food cake," she explained, "but not with chocolate icing."

On the one-year anniversary of Larry Jr.'s passing, I attended a mass held in his memory. The church was filled to capacity, and there was not even room to stand.

To me it seemed as if Larry had written the mass himself, including little jokes and wonderful memories throughout the service. I believe that he wanted to be remembered by everyone, even those like myself who didn't know him well, and he communicated with us from the other side with joyful laughter.

The next day, one of AnnMarie's co-workers brought in a cake, placed it on her desk and announced, "It's an angel food cake."

When the box was opened, AnnMarie looked at the chocolate icing with wide eyes and recalled what her son had predicted about the icing in a message to me several months earlier. It was as if Larry Jr. was thanking his mother for the wonderful memorial service.

Sometimes when I relay a message from the spirit world, it does not necessarily mean that the message will come true that day, or month. Sometimes it may take years. Little Larry's father told me, "It is strange that with all the pain we have been through with the loss of our son, I believe more in God now than I ever have. If you could only see the people's faces as you are delivering messages to each person. The smiles and tears reflect an overwhelming gratefulness to have those precious communications."

The Wish

As I was working with a woman named Tina, her daughter who had died more than two years earlier came forth.

"Your daughter tells me how difficult it has been on you since her passing," I told Tina. "She wants you to know she is fine. She wants me to tell you that you should start enjoying your life. Tina, she hands you a bouquet of roses and wishes you a happy birthday."

With tears running down her face, Tina said, "Today is my birthday."

"Your daughter is with her grandmother," I added. "This woman speaks of pain in her hand."

Then as often happens when I'm bringing messages in, my fingers suddenly appeared to be crippled. Tina looked at my hands and said, "That is how my mom's hands used to get."

"Tina, your mom says thank you for all the prayers."

Tina hugged and kissed me and thanked me profusely. She claimed communion with her daughter through me made her birthday the best ever.

≈⊶⊙⊷≈

I donate two nights a month to the groups that attend the Institute of Creative Healing. There are several groups that are a part of the Institute's program: psychic development, yoga and meditation. The most difficult yet most rewarding experience is my work with the bereavement group.

I highly recommend that anyone who has lost a loved one join a bereavement group. Each person in the group is going through a range of emotions as he or she copes with loss. Voicing your feelings helps the healing process. Of course, the work I do that eases the grieving process is to bring forth a love one who has passed over. It is comforting and strengthening to the bereaved person to know that her relative or friend is in the safe keeping of God.

The questions asked by the grieving usually are predictable: "Is my loved one okay?" "Is he angry about the way he left earthplane?"

Interestingly, I have never brought forth anyone who is unhappy in the other dimension.

I have heard apologies from those who've gone over for things they may have caused while they were on the earthplane. And I've witnessed repeatedly the peace, love and everlasting tranquility that comes to the departed after they've passed on.

I found a profound and moving message printed on a memorial card in a chapel. It is reproduced here. I think it is appropriate to read and reread this lovely poem when you think of your loved ones who have gone on. I am sorry to say that I do not know the name of the author:

To Those I Love

When I am gone, release me, let me go. I have so many things to see and do.

You mustn't tie yourself to me with tears, be happy that we had so many years.

I gave you my love. You can only guess how much you gave me in happiness.

But now it's time I traveled on alone.

So grieve awhile for me if grieve you must, then let your grief be comforted by trust.

It's only for a while that we must part, so bless the memories within your heart.

I won't be far away, for life goes on. So if you need me, call and I will come.

Though you can't see or touch me, I'll be near,

And if you listen with your heart you'll hear, all of my love around you soft and clear.

And then when you must come this way alone, I'll greet you with a smile and say, "Welcome Home."

⚜

One of the most touching stories I ever heard was about a beloved mother who departed, leaving behind a gift of love that forever would be remembered by her son and his wife.

This marvelous anecdote came to me from my publisher, Ursula Bacon, with the note that it would later be part of a new book in preparation, but was perfect, she thought, for *Just a Breath Away*. It proves how love can survive death and separation and leave an eternal message of affection that time can never erase. I include it here with her permission.

A Gift Beyond Time

I'm sure everybody heard at least a few of those uncomplimentary mother-in-law jokes which were popular for a while in the sixties and seventies. Their bad-taste endings rarely left a shred of goodness in the mother-in-law image. In the case of my own mother-in-law, I was lucky. She didn't fit the punch lines.

My mother-in-law was Mary, and she was a proper lady. The southern lilt in her voice made even a harsh word sound like a caress, and her off-the-wall feminine logic seemed related to the aphorisms of Gracie Allen of radio and early television fame, whose husband, George Burns, played the straight man.

Mary was all of five foot four, had a youthful figure, a set of legs that would bring tears of envy to a chorus girl's eyes, and a heart the size of Texas —and that's BIG! Her generosity was only exceeded by her blindness to the faults of others. God gave us unconditional love, my mother-in-law perfected it.

During most of her marriage, she had faithfully followed her husband from one US Navy post to the next, setting up house at the drop of a hat, raising two boys and a girl along the way. Her husband was a no-nonsense man of stern behavior and a noticeable lack of self-esteem. He fought his own dark shadows which spilled over into the family life as overly strict military discipline. He ran the house with an iron fist. There was little encouragement for laughter or friendly banter, and social contact with other people was lacking. Mary, on the other hand, was gentle —

although feisty when necessary — and eased her husband's harsh ways with add-on love and lighthearted words.

When the children left home, Mary in a sense left home as well. She worked herself into a prestigious position in a family-held oil company in San Antonio, which gave her the economic freedom to do what she liked to do best: bestow gifts, do those extra "little" things for her children and grandchildren, and come to their rescue when they most needed help. What's a mother for? Mary had a clever way of folding a twenty-dollar bill into a small square and slipping it secretly into a grandchild's hand, into a greeting card or into a Christmas stocking. Her generosity to her family knew no boundaries and was limited only by the restrictions of her bank account. And, even then, she managed to perform miracles. There was nothing too small or too big to tackle when it came to "he'ppin' out the children."

Her husband died when Mary was sixty-seven, and eight years later she finally retired. It was in the early seventies that I married her oldest son and consequently met Mary. My husband and I were working on a publishing project in Montana when she decided to visit. We liked each other almost instantly, and at the end of her stay with us and for the rest of her life a deep bond of mutual love and respect kept us in each other's hearts. When she no longer wanted to keep house, she lived with her daughter during the winter and came to us to spend the summers.

It was during those summers that I really got to know Mary and watched in amazement how she overlooked everyone's flaws and was able to remove herself from serious problems with no more effort than shooing a pesky fly off a piece of Southern-fried chicken. Typically, she would summarize her philosophy of dealing with problems with a smile on her face and a drawl that gave emphasis to her statement, "Why darlin', nothin's important enough to fuss over and lose sleep. It all comes to pass, it doesn't come to stay." Who can argue with Southern wisdom?

She told me stories of her growing up in a little town on the Pamlico Sound in North Carolina where her ancestors had settled. Her descriptions brought to life that unique, independent spirit which belonged solely to that part of America. She personified the kind of grace, charm and down-home humor I refer to as "those irresistible Southern ways." I had grown up in Europe and China and couldn't have presented a life more in contrast to hers. She listened with equal fascination to my tales — two different generations from entirely different backgrounds — two women talking LIFE.

The summer Mary visited us in Montana found my husband and me deeply involved in our work and we took little time off for ourselves. Mary knew how much her son liked to go fishing and was forever urging him to "run along and catch a fish for supper." Many times she'd push one of her cleverly folded twenties in my hand, insist that I pack a picnic lunch and go off to some wild stream under the Big Sky where the rainbows would be waiting for us.

Somehow, grateful as we were for her reminders that we should entertain ourselves, as well as work, we never got away, and before we knew it, it was fall and time for her to return to her winter home in Texas.

I could not help but notice, almost with surprise, as I assisted Mary with her packing, that the years were catching up with my mother-in-law. She was getting quite frail and fragile. I wanted to hug her to me and whisper, "Stop the clock, stay young for me, for both of us."

We took her to the airport and we said our good-byes.

As I watched her slight figure walk slowly away from us and disappear into the belly of the big jet, a fleeting moment of bottomless sadness engulfed me. I knew I wasn't going to see her again. She died before the year was out.

Our work in Montana came to an end and, a few days before our return to Oregon, we decided to go fishing in the Bitterroot for the last time. I opened the big tackle box we hadn't used for a long time to check if we needed anything. Taped to the inner lid of the tackle box was a white envelope addressed to both of us. It was in Mary's handwriting. My heart missed a beat as I carefully lifted the tape that held the envelope in place, and opened it.

When I unfolded the white note paper, one of Mary's twenty-dollar bills folded in a neat square spilled out. Through a veil of tears, I read the note in her fine handwriting:

You must be going fishing if you read this.
Have a good time and catch a big one for supper.
Love, Mother

I love Mary's story because it represents a mother's wisdom and understanding of the value of connection between one another. Of course, it seems obvious in the reading that Mary left her gift to her son and daughter-in-law as a parting gesture, a reminder of the love she felt for the two she was leaving behind. She must have known that her time on earth was coming to an end, and in the bigness of her heart she wrote the note as a tangible link between the living and the departed — for surely she was deeply aware that her note would not be discovered until after she died.

There is a more profound meaning to Mary's story than its sentimental appeal and that refers to the subject of the last chapter of this book — How Death Teaches Us

About Life. It is probably the most important chapter because it examines how death gradually has been removed from family life when for generations before it was regarded as an inevitable presence which drew families closer together and taught them to more appreciate the joy of living. The rituals that surrounded death helped to teach survivors how to feel about death and how to relate themselves to the long parade of ancestors who had lived before and to future relatives who would live and die after them. Such a perspective gave family members a greater sense of spiritual security, a strong feeling of position and place in the long drama of generations, and faith that their own ending would be but a new beginning and a reunion with loved ones gone before.

I think the reader will find strong interest in the final chapter and, perhaps, ideas that will help her or him arrive at a more satisfactory relationship with the idea of death.

Chapter 25

Learning About Life from Death

A long time ago, people were more intimate with death and they believed in miracles. Today, even as our population grows older, we are more oriented to youth than to preparation for dying. Certainly, that cannot be bad, because it reflects our prolonged vigor, a mental attitude that attainment of sixty or seventy or eighty years of age does not mean the individual should curl up like a shrunken leaf, withdraw from life and wait for death to come.

The fact is we are indeed living, physically adept, to much older ages, far in advance of our most recent forebears. More than half of our national population is over fifty and aging fast.

If there ever was a time in America when we should look to our philosophy about death, it is now. For as we have become more modern, more technologically advanced, it seems as though we have distanced ourselves from the grief ceremonies and memorial observations we once conducted to see a loved one into the next world. These ceremonies were held to formally say good-bye, and on a deeper level to reestablish our personal identity as a member of a related cluster of humans who had a common ancestral root.

It is this tradition of death observances and celebrations that is largely missing today, depriving us of a crucial and valuable link with those who have gone on.

Think about that, please. It is our link with our parents, uncles, aunts, grandparents, the heroes, villains, explorers and pioneers who populated the past that gives us strong definition, colors our character and plants in us genes of greatness, foolishness, love, mercy and vision. Our progenitors gave us personal history, ideas, courage and inspiration.

Thus, it is sad, and makes us less effective as humans, to be cut off from the death process which makes up the past with its vanished men and women of significance or mediocrity, individuals from whom we gained our varied inheritances.

It was Eda LeShan, in her book *Learning to Say Good-By*, who captured our modern dilemma of preferred isolation from death:

"Gradually, death became more removed from daily life. Few people died at home. Mostly it was old people who died. Children and parents could live for long periods of time without ever hearing about the death of someone they loved. Unhappily, no generation has ever lived without hearing about people dying in wars, and there have been terrible wars in the last few generations. But in spite of this, the fact of death was seen and talked about less and less. It was almost as if people thought that if no one talked about death, maybe it would just go away.

"During this period, parents were inclined to protect their children — they did not take them to funerals, they tried not to cry or show their grief in front of their children, and they did not talk to them about dying.

"Recently, people have begun to realize that such attitudes were very foolish. When a death occurred, neither grownups nor children had any idea what to do or even how to feel. And since death had been treated as something too ugly and terrible ever to mention, people who were dying were often very lonely. Nobody would let them talk about their fears; nobody would ever say an honest good-by. And many children grew up feeling very embarrassed about death, not knowing how to act or what to say. They wondered about death but were afraid to ask any questions."

To a large extent, but perhaps for different reasons — chiefly the growing impersonality in our society which distances us from neighbors as well as our own relatives — many of us still do not seem to know how or what to say about death. We do feel embarrassed and uncomfortable about death, and because it is alien to us, when it should not be, we shun opportunities to find out about it, a conclusion in life which, inevitably, each of us will face.

In the previous chapter I told the story of Mary, who left a singular and touching note for her son and daughter-in-law to be found after she died.

Now, from another friend comes a true story about death which I think illustrates the normal curiosity of children about dying and how its impression on the young can bring home the important lesson playwright George Bernard Shaw taught when he wrote, "Heartbreak is life educating us."

The Girl in the Funeral Home

When I was nine years old, I and some other boys who lived in East San Diego used to play baseball on the sandy diamond at our grammar school.

At one end of the diamond, across an alleyway, there were several buildings whose rear entrances faced the school yard. There was a drugstore, a five-and-dime, a small grocery, a hardware store, and on the corner was a funeral home.

I can't remember which of the boys on our baseball team told us that a pretty teen-age girl had died and was lying in her casket in the viewing room of the funeral home.

Immediately all of us were fascinated and curious about the dead girl. Not one of us had ever attended a funeral. I, for one, had never seen a dead person. In those days television was still a miracle that was just starting up and there were no pictures of dead or dying people to educate us. Another decade would pass before the new visual journalism would present us with images of living and dying that startled and horrified us.

As children sometimes do, the group of us standing on the baseball diamond that late, sunny afternoon made an unusual decision. We agreed to knock at the front door of the funeral home and politely ask for permission to view the dead girl.

There were six of us on our team, laden with baseball gloves, two wooden bats and a catcher's mask, who waited at the impressive black-painted front door of the funeral home with its discreet bright brass nameplate above the shiny door handle.

We could hear the chimes of the doorbell ring distantly in the interior, announcing our presence, and soon approaching footsteps. Facing us when the door swung open was a tall man with bushy eyebrows and a stern face. He was dressed in a sharply pressed dark suit. He looked at us in surprise, then said, "What can I do for you, boys?"

I had been selected as spokesman and I said with a dry mouth, "Sir, we found out that a girl has died and you have her here. We don't know her name, but we wondered ... well ... if we could see her?"

The solemn expression on the man's face seemed to melt away as he examined each of us with his probing eyes. His dark gaze seemed to strip away our courage and laid bare our innocence. Like the others, I wished I were anyplace but where I was standing.

In a soft voice, he said, "None of you has ever seen a dead person, is that right?"

"Yes, sir," we all mumbled. I think every one of us at that moment felt foolish, a little frightened at the impulse that had taken us on such a strange errand. I know that I felt a prickle of shame to have presented myself to the immaculate stranger in a dusty sweatshirt, scuffed tennis shoes and faded jeans. I desperately wanted to escape.

But suddenly, with a warm smile, the man swung the door open wider. "Come on in, boys," he said. "Leave your baseball gear in the hallway."

Astonished and subdued, all of us entered the funeral home, deposited our gloves, balls and bats on a wooden bench in the hallway, and followed our escort across the soundless carpet into a softly lighted room. In one corner, surrounded by a faint pink glow of indirect lighting, was a white casket, lined with rose satin that fell into smooth, straight folds to the carpeted floor.

Our tall guardian of the dead beckoned to me with his finger and I was the first to look upon the face and form of a lovely girl, about sixteen, who lay as though asleep, on her cushion of satin. Her thick, brown hair, arranged around her oval face in a half halo, framed her features with a soft focus.

Her loveliness took my breath away. Her lips were lightly painted with lipstick and her closed eyes were shaded delicately with a faint blue overtone. Her skin was lightly powdered and her cheekbones were colored with a rose blush. She appeared to be asleep, but there was a final stillness about her form that convinced me that I would never see her modest breasts rise and fall with inspiration. She was dressed in a plain, white silk gown, with a row of covered buttons ranging from the soft, rounded collar that circled her neck and descended to her waist. Her hands and arms were folded against her chest, crossing at the wrists, in the typical arrangement that indicated final rest, although I did not know that at the time.

I stared at the girl for perhaps two or three minutes, long enough to sense the impatience of the boys standing behind me, waiting for their turn to look at death in a lovely form.

After I awkwardly whispered "Thank you" to the kindly funeral director, who had been standing quietly near the head of the casket, I walked slowly into the hallway where we had left our baseball gear. I tried to understand what my confused feelings were, but my one overwhelming emotion was immense awe mixed with regret. And beneath that, as though the ache in my heart was like a deep well filled with sorrow and loss, there was an engulfing sadness.

I remember also that as I stood alone waiting in the hallway for the others, a hymn from my mother's church popped into my head. It was "The Old Rugged Cross" and from that moment on, whenever I heard that sad refrain, I associated it with the dead girl and the lump that formed in my throat.

My eyes were moist with unshed tears and I fought to keep them inside me, because it wasn't manly to cry and show weakness to the others.

We all dispersed quickly and set out for home on our separate paths, with no conversation, except, "See ya later." I assumed correctly that each of my teammates was overwhelmed. They, no more than I, could talk about the lovely girl who should have grown to maturity, married, had children and died when she was an old lady.

For many years after visiting the girl in her casket, I dreamed and wondered about her, caught in an eternal sleep from which she would never open her eyes.

I never told anybody in my family about our visit to the funeral home. I did not wish to share my private thoughts, because I had not come to a conclusion about my own attitude toward death.

I thought about dying from time to time in the years after I saw the girl, but because my immediate family was intact, death wasn't a morbid happening that threatened me, my parents, or my brother and sister.

When my grandfather died in North Carolina, probably a year or so after my visit to the funeral home, and my mother flew east to his wake, I was very little affected because we children did not know him well. I remembered him mistily as a tall, affable man who smoked a pipe and had the aroma of Prince Albert tobacco in his clothes, and who poured his breakfast coffee into a saucer so that he could blow it cool with his breath.

I learned eventually that death is an event for which we must prepare and that meant developing a personal philosophy of life, one which took me many years to formulate.

✿❀✿

As my friend indicated, formulating a philosophy about life and death is important for the reasons I listed early in this chapter, but I think it is worthwhile now to consider what you may do to keep the memory of a loved one alive so that the continuity of your immediate and extended family can be preserved for future children.

After a lifetime of thinking about death, listening to voices from the other side, counseling grieving survivors to accept their loss and move forward, and witnessing spirits who have made appearances after the death of their bodies, I have come up with four suggestions that readers may wish to apply to their lives when they are facing the death of a loved one.

These suggestions also form the basis of information parents can call upon to educate their children about dying.

1. Start a Chart of Your Family's Personal History.

If you capture your parents' and grandparents' memories and recollections of their past, you will have created a "living" biography from which your family history can be constructed.

This is not a new idea, but it becomes more important today because the old-fashioned family has deteriorated. We are not as close to cousins, aunts and uncles, even parents and grandparents as we used to be. That is unfortunate, for as a result of our isolation and separateness we have lost contact with our family heritages.

It is comforting, satisfying and stabilizing to have a sense of who we came from. To know that Great-Great-

Uncle Joe was a blackbirder, a slave trader who proriteu from human cargoes sold at auction may be disturbing, but his black deeds may be balanced on the scales of your family history by courageous men and women who saved lives in the Civil War.

The point is, your past is rich in human anecdotes, in love, hate and forgiveness — part of the vigorous human stream. Not to know them — the heroes and villains — and the parts your parents and grandparents played in the long drama is to make folly of death and to forever lose vital links in the human trail that contributed to who you are.

Never forget that your mother and father, and their parents before them, were different from anyone else in the world. That's right, they were one of a kind, just as you are, an individual who is his own unique design. It is because of that uniqueness that the heartbreak of having a parent, or a child, or a grandparent die is so devastating. Such deaths teach us how valuable a human can be. Because each one of us is special, one of a kind, one who can never come again in the same pattern, we feel the death of the one is so terribly painful. Other people may find our love, but each love is a star that shines with a very special light in our heart.

It can be a real effort to get parents and grandparents to dig into the past to reveal who they have been and to describe their own parents and grandparents. But there are no other sources from which you gain valuable information if they pass on and leave an empty silence behind.

I've discovered a tape recorder is an easy method to get parents and grandparents to talk and reminisce, to remember events and actions that come to the surface with a little prodding from you.

2. Teach Your Children What You Have Learned About Death. Make them understand that is is as much a part of life as breathing. If you believe in an afterlife, explain your views to them. You may wish to use the Holy Bible, or the Koran or the Torah as a reference point, depending on your religious persuasion.

Do not allow your children to form a viewpoint about death from television. Almost unfailingly, television provides false and misleading ideas about death by promoting programs of violence and callousness in depictions of death. Children may adopt such ideas as these, and if uncorrected, they become a twisted interpretation of how to view life and death.

3. For Those of You Who Are More Adventuresome, you may wish to consult a genuine psychic or clairvoyant who can introduce you to the world beyond the grave. Always ask for references and check the reputation of any psychic you may use.

In the same general category of the spiritual are respected masters who teach meditation, centering and a variety of methods to learn to go inside to contact the "genius within" — the God of the Universe who is present in each of us. Such revelations, as you may discover, will certainly alter your previous ideas about dying.

4. Finally, Learn How to Grieve and teach your children by example. There are several good books on grieving. One I can strongly recommend is *Death: The Final Stage of Growth*, by Elisabeth Kübler-Ross.

My bereavement work has brought me in contact with many people who have lost children, parents, brothers and sisters. Sometimes the person is newly aggrieved and sometimes he may have lost a loved one many years earlier, and is suffering a deep wound of loss that does not seem to heal. I find it a heart-warming experience to witness the expression of such a person when he realizes that the messages I bring from across the chasm actually come from the loved one he is pining for.

My method, of course, is very nontraditional. But I have discovered that if the survivors are convinced their missing ones are happy in their new lives, their grief abates, replaced with awe and wonder.

Sometimes after we lose someone, guilt sets in. Did we do enough for the absent loved one in her final days?

I deeply believe that through the agonizing process of grief, each prayer offered is certainly a way of helping a loved one passed over and to help ourselves adjust. Many times I have heard those on the other side admonish a family member to move forward, to remember happy times and to forget the anguish or pain the deceased went through just before his passing.

It is terribly difficult to watch someone we love leave the earthplane, or to know that he is going to be leaving shortly. I have learned that it helps the dying person on his voyage for us to express love and appreciation for him, and to assure him that his final decision to leave is one that we must not hinder by our own deep sense of impending loss.

The emotional tears we cannot hide are needed to release our anxiety and anger and to cope with the impending loss. Just as the ocean was created with salt and can heal our wounds, so can the salt of our tears help us recover from grief.

I believe that when we enter the earthplane, just before our first breath, we are given the secrets of life and the choice to accept or reject them. As we take our first breath, we begin the process of death; it is always just a breath away.

About the Author

Reverend Edward N. Tabbitas

Edward Tabbitas was born with a designated path and followed each new path with determination and stride. From the age of seven he has been able to communicate with the spiritual realm. He is able to reach into the dimensions of the spirit world and bring forth loved ones who have passed over. His dedication comes from his love of fellow humans and his desire to help ease their pain and anguish during the loss of a loved one. His mission is to act as a communication relay between the boundaries of life and death, and also to bring a sense of comfort and understanding to the bereaved by peeking beyond the veil in their behalf.

To order additional copies of

Just a Breath Away

Book: $14.95   Shipping/Handling $3.50

Contact: ***BookPartners, Inc.***
P.O. Box 922, Wilsonville, OR 97070
Fax: 503-682-8684
Phone 503-682-9821
Phone: 1-800-895-7323